PRIMERO DIOS

PRIMERO DIOS

Alcoholics Anonymous
and the Hispanic Community

Kenneth G. Davis, O.F.M., Conv.

SUP

Selinsgrove: Susquehanna University Press
London and Toronto: Associated University Presses

Associated University Presses
440 Forsgate Drive
Cranbury, NJ 08512

Associated University Presses
25 Sicilian Avenue
London WC1A 2QH, England

Associated University Presses
P.O. Box 338, Port Credit
Mississauga, Ontario
Canada L5G 4L8

HN
5278
D38
1994

The paper used in this publication meets the requirements
of the American National Standard for Permanence of Paper
for Printed Library Materials Z39.48-1984.

Library of Congress Cataloging-in-Publication Data

Davis, Kenneth G., 1957–
    Primero Dios : Alcoholics Anonymous and the Hispanic community /
Kenneth G. Davis.
        p.   cm.
    Includes bibliographical references and index.
    ISBN 0-945636-50-4 (alk. paper)
    1. Alcoholics Anonymous.   2. Mexican Americans—Alcohol use.
3. Mexican Americans—Rehabilitation.   4. Alcoholism—Treatment—
United States.   5. Alcoholism—Religious aspects—Catholic Church.
I. Title.
HV5278.D38   1994
362.29'286'08972073—dc20   92-51000
                                                            CIP

PRINTED IN THE UNITED STATES OF AMERICA

Contents

Preface

MARGARITA B. MELVILLE

Kenneth Davis, a Franciscan priest with hands-on experience in a Spanish-speaking community, through observation, study, and praxis, has developed a theoretical and realistic approach to introduce the philosophy and practice of Alcoholics Anonymous to Catholic pastoral agents. When he came to see me about doing a second reading course on Mexican-American culture as preparation, I readily agreed. He was fluent in Spanish and at that time was working actively with Mexican-Americans in his parish. He read voraciously and we discussed avidly. What was abstract and theoretical in the texts he read was translated and expanded by the day-to-day life experiences of parishioners, relatives, and their friends. We shared facts, insights, and perceptions. One of the major problems facing many of the men and their families was alcoholism.

Father Davis thought that the program of Alcoholics Anonymous, with its twelve steps, resonated with popular Catholicism. He presents here the theoretical and sociological background to understanding A.A. and Mexican-American culture. This became the background to a handbook he wrote in Spanish as a tool for those who want to understand and work with Mexican-American alcoholics.* In it he explains and develops the twelve steps of A.A. in terms applicable to use with Mexican-American Catholics so that pastoral agents from the same community can learn to use A.A. as a resource to help those who so badly need it. Testing the handbook he wrote in Spanish to inculturate the A.A. process to Mexican-Americans produced its share of expected frustrations that accompany cross-cultural work. These are bound to arise

---

*See *Cuando el Tomar Ya No Es Gozar* (Los Angeles: Franciscan Communications, 1993).

despite understanding, sensitivity, and the conscious effort to avoid them. The analysis of that process is itself instructive and can serve as a model for other types of applications.

The outcome is presented here. It is a report of the sociological and theoretical basis and the research results that needed to be shared and circulated. This is a practical study, one that responds to a felt need. This is not for the ivory tower and a dusty library shelf. It is for the use of those willing to be involved and to chip away at the often inadvertent racism or ethnocentrism to which we are all prone.

Many Mexican-Americans find themselves culturally alienated. They live outside the economic mainstream in social backwaters that offer little more than doubtful survival. Their supervisors and bosses relate to them with northern coldness or employ attitudes of class difference in order to distance themselves. The search for work sometimes takes Mexican-Americans to locations where their social relations are limited to other single men or to a nuclear family far from other relatives. When Mexican-Americans go to church, they often find that the liturgy is designed for an English-speaking congregation that is most comfortable in an unemotional, more anonymous scene. In all these settings, solace and camaraderie often involve the excessive consumption of alcohol. Slavery to alcohol is too often the result. This is a major health hazard and a family-destroyer of serious proportions in Mexican-American communities.

When a harsh, competitive society foments self-doubt and a sense of inadequacy and powerlessness, the recovery of one's pride and self-worth through faith and brotherhood can be a strong antidote. A.A. provides a well-proven map of the path to conversion and recovery. Davis analyzes and compares the dynamics of conversion and recovery from the perspectives both of Catholic Mexican-Americans and of the A.A. philosophy and finds their nexus.

The use of the idea and methodology of A.A. in a Catholic setting is not new. Jesuit Ed Dowling endorsed it in 1947 after meeting the founder, Bill Wilson. Dowling saw the parallels of the twelve steps with the Spiritual Exercises of Saint Ignatius. Both are concerned with regeneration, with taking strength in the face of weakness, with deciding to lift up oneself by reaching out to a supernatural power. What is new here is the proposal to adapt this philosophy and practice specifically to Mexican-American Catholics.

The analysis of the beliefs about death and death rituals among Mexican-Americans is an appropriate choice to illustrate the contrast of their culture with that of the Anglo mainstream. The reader will garner insights into Mexican-American culture that are valuable in themselves and that go beyond the purpose of adapting the A.A. philosophy. Davis demonstrates the sensitivity and insight of a pastor who accompanies his parishioners through the vicissitudes of life, but who also looks beyond the apparent to the underlying patterns of behavior.

The account here of the development of a Spanish-language, practical handbook is a description of a careful and sensitive application of the A.A. system to the values and characteristics of Mexican-American culture. It also provides a working design of a methodology for the creation of other parish and community programs in multicultural settings. The recognition by pastors and social workers that we all have a tendency to formulate ethnocentric designs and plans will help them avoid the failure of conceiving well-meaning but shortsighted plans. Sometimes failures are blamed on the lack of good will, interest, or understanding when, in fact, a design may not have been properly adapted to culturally-based values and perceptions. I welcome this valuable study and analysis. I anticipate that a sizable population of Mexican-American Catholics will greatly benefit from its circulation.

Acknowledgements

First, kudos to kin: All of my family, especially my sisters, have nurtured me in countless ways, and as such are the true authors of all my work. My nephews and nieces, as surrogate children to me, are a beloved blessing.

Joseph Angelini helped as proofreader. Thanks also to the librarians of the Alcohol Research Group, the Graduate Theological Union, and the University of California at Berkeley for their invaluable assistance. Special mention must be made of Dr. Carmen María Cervantes Ed.D. and Mr. Vicente Mejía for their kind advice and support. The entire Conventual Franciscan Province of Our Lady of Consolation was instrumental in this work; most especially Wayne Hellmann, who instilled in me a love of learning and a desire to serve.

Lastly, I would like to express my gratitude to all those who have allowed me into their lives as a minister of Faith.

I dedicate this book to my mother, Viola L. Davis, in profound gratitude and lasting love, for her having dedicated her life to me.

A chapter of this book was published under the title "A Return to the Roots: Conversion and the Culture of the Mexican-Descent" in the January 1992 issue of *Pastoral Psychology,* and is reprinted here with permission from the Human Sciences Press.

Permission has been granted by the University of California Press for material quoted from Arthur Kleinman, *Patients and Healers in the Context of Culture.* Copyright © 1980 The Regents of the University of California.

Permission has been granted to the author for material quoted from "Conversion, Culture, and Cognitive Categories" by Paul G. Hiebert, from *Gospel in Context* 1, no. 4 (1978).

Introduction:
On Being a Frog in my Field

The voice of the mercurial main character in C. S. Lewis's novel *The Screwtape Letters* drips with disgust as he refers to humans as "amphibians," that is, a mongrel mix of body and soul. He is evilly eloquent in explaining how even the animals (unsouled bodies) are more worthy than humans, since at least they are pure creatures, not a mixture of body and soul.

With each passing day, I feel more like the frog which Screwtape endeavors to tempt and destroy, not because of any platonic division between body and soul, but rather because I am a cultural amphibian, navigating between two different and often inimical worlds.

First there is the world of my birth. I am a white, middle-class anglophone (i.e., one whose first and predominant language is English) from a part of the country where Hispanics are known only from Frito Lay bags. However, this is also a Catholic world, and I am influenced by my decision to become a Franciscan and a priest. As such, I have always striven to minister to those in the Church who are poor and marginated,[1] and at this time in this country that includes those Catholics of Mexican descent.

Therefore, I began some ten years ago to study Spanish, and then later the various Hispanic cultures.[2] The peculiarity of the United States Catholic Church, however, is that none of these cultures exists in isolation. We are a mosaic (sometimes a mess!) of various persons of color (e.g., African-Americans, Filipinos, Vietnamese, Mexicans, Chicanos) and anglophone Caucasians. The Catholic ethos holds that all God's children should live placidly under a single roof: The reality is that we get along about as well as a gaggle of brats.

As I have written elsewhere, this reality forced me to face the ignorance of many Catholics (lay, religious, and ordained) concerning this multicultural reality, as well as the sin of racism that

13

exists among us.³ Since I work with Hispanics, I have sometimes been labelled "the spic priest," and I labor without the camaraderie and support available to priests of my own cultural background who minister to "their own." As an African-American friend so delicately explained, "You've been a white man in a white man's world. You're used to saying jump and all the world says, 'how high?' But now that you're a spic-lover, you're worse than us—you're a traitor to 'your own.'"

So the one world I struggle to live in is the one of my birth: one I know and love but that I can condone only up to a point, and one that sometimes doesn't accept me at all.

The other world I have entered is the Mexican-descent world, where I am also an outsider. After nine years of working with Hispanics, and two years into my doctoral program, focused specifically on ministry to people of Mexican descent, a well-known Chicana religious bluntly asked me: "Why don't you go work with your own people?" Professionals in this world are often blunt. Lay persons tend to be more patient, but even on my best days I know that I walk this world oblivious to the subtlety of the *indirecta*, unaware of the significance of gestures, slang, and tones of speech.

I'm a frog in my field. My chosen field is the ministerial priesthood, specifically among those of Mexican descent. Among my brother priests (predominantly white anglophones) I never feel totally at home, yet among those I am dedicated to serving I also continue to be acutely aware that I shall never belong.

I use the term "frog" for various reasons. First, for its levity. I do not feel sorry for myself, nor blame anyone for the experience I describe. Despite its difficulties, it is my choice, and has afforded opportunities and joys that far outweigh any pain. Second, I hesitate to draw parallels to what Hispanic Catholics (à la Elizondo) describe as the mestizo experience (being caught between two cultures).⁴ While I understand their struggle, and to a certain degree share it, my own struggle is quite different. I have a choice. I can fade back into the dominant world and live blissfully forever after. Chicanos and others have no such choice. Their experience is different in kind, not just degree, and I do not intend to denigrate it with cheap empathy.

Nevertheless, I continue to try to navigate between these two worlds. Such dexterity requires critical reflection on the culture of my birth, as well as critical reflection on the Hispanic cultures. Such reflection is based on the Catholic Faith. When I say that racism is a sin, I do so because I am consciously judging my own culture by the standards of the Faith.

Critically reflecting on my own culture is a skill I have used since I first studied philosophy some fifteen years ago. It continues to occupy me, but it is an ability that I comfortably do intellectually, if not always emotionally.

Critical reflection on Hispanic cultures (specifically those of Mexican descent) in light of the Faith is a skill I lack. It is also an enterprise that must always be done in community, i.e. with, by, and for the members of this culture. The goal of my ministry has been therefore to follow Ernie Cortes's iron rule: NEVER DO FOR PEOPLE WHAT THEY CAN DO FOR THEMSELVES.[5] I hope to share in the critical self-reflection of this community in light of the Faith, in order to better serve it as a minister of the Faith. For the purpose of this book, I have chosen one small but urgent and important area for reflection: the treatment of alcoholism among the male, Mexican-descent, Catholic population.

The book is constructed using the now familiar VER (look), JUZGAR (judge), ACTUAR (act), EVALUAR (evaluate) strategy of liberation theology.

Chapter 1 looks at the reality of alcoholism among the Mexican-descent population in the United States, and at Alcoholics Anonymous (A.A.) as a possible treatment modality for this population. As this chapter explains, one reason I feel A.A. holds promise for this population is precisely because it respects the iron rule. A.A. insists on being financially independent, and is based on mutuality, not on professional-client dependence. However, this chapter also questions whether A.A. can be truly inculturated into the Mexican-descent, Catholic (MDC) community. Since conversion is the key to A.A., I identify that concept as the essential one to be examined in the quest for inculturation.[6]

Chapters 2 and 3 therefore judge conversion first from an MDC perspective (drawing on popular spirituality), and then from the perspective of A.A. I conclude that indeed the dynamics of conversion are remarkably similar in both contexts.

Chapter 4 then recounts my attempt to ACTUAR, that is, to act upon this information. My project was to attempt to teach a group of self-identified pastoral agents in the Church about alcoholism and A.A. If A.A. is to be inculturated in the MDC community, these are the persons who have the unique opportunity to do so.

Chapter 5 evaluates this attempt, and suggests ways that would have improved it, as well as areas still in need of further research. The fruit of this work is being separately published by Franciscan Communications Press under the title *Cuando El Tomar Ya No Es Gozar*. A conclusion, bibliography, and appendixes complete my study.

PRIMERO DIOS

1

A.A.: Making It User Friendly

The purpose of this chapter is to examine the efficacy of Alcoholics Anonymous (A.A.) as a treatment modality for the male alcoholic of Mexican descent living in the United States of America. It is limited to this population both because it is the U.S. Hispanic group most thoroughly researched, and because this research identifies it as a group at high risk for alcoholism.[1] The chapter has three parts: (1) to identify and describe this alcoholic; (2) to explore treatment possibilities for this identified patient, especially that offered by A.A.; and (3) to clarify the role of the pastoral agent in this treatment process.

Identifying the Alcoholic

A review of the literature shows that acculturation is positively associated with drinking problems, although this association is more nuanced and convoluted among males than among females.[2]

Among acculturated men, heavy drinking begins to be problematic around age thirty. At that time there is a decrease in abstention and an increase in frequent, heavy drinking. As the men grow older, there is some reversal in this pattern, with the net result being a more neutral stance toward alcohol. However, a marginalized group of heavy drinkers does not participate in this reversal, but rather begins to exhibit signs of alcoholism.[3] Anecdotal reports to the contrary, the notion of "machismo" is not a determining factor with this group. Indeed, a close examination shows the positive influence of machismo. The cultural myth of the macho is that he is a responsible man, one whose drinking does not interfere with either his stature in the community or his position as family provider. This is what differentiates him from the alcoholic and labels the latter deviant.[4] The "low-bottom" alcoholic male does not reflect the macho myth—rather, he becomes marginated from his own community precisely because he deviates from accepted drinking practices. A marginated male can be accurately diagnosed as alcoholic when he becomes violent or sexually belligerent, fails to reciprocate help from friends and extended family, languishes in his role as provider (due to health or employment problems), and when his wife or children try to contain or control his drinking. These are all symptoms of his having exceeded the drinking customs of his particular community. One earns the right to drink because one fulfills the cultural role of a man; one deviates from accepted drinking practices when drinking eclipses this role.[5] A profile of this identified patient then is:

> An acculturated thirty- to sixty-year-old who is marginated from both the dominant and the Mexican-American community. He is marginated because he deviates from Mexican-American male drinking patterns which correlate responsible manhood with responsible drinking. However, he probably retains some social stability because his immediate family continues to support him.[6]

Treatment Possibilities

Almost nothing is being done for this identified alcoholic. Very little research is available in order to design a prevention-education program that is culturally sensitive. The problem of institutionalized injustice and how it relates to such minority health problems is almost completely ignored.[7] These related issues are important but distinct from treatment. The most germane question for this chapter is: Are conventional treatment programs effective for this population? The answer is no. The reasons are two.

First, the Mexican-American culture has its own alternate support system, a matrix of extended family, fictive kin (e.g., *padrinos*), *carnales* (friends so close they are "of one flesh"), and a religious family (not only a Church, but a felt relation to the *mysterium tremendum* of Life).[8] Therefore when a Mexican-American experiences a problem, it is only natural that he turns to this nurturing network for a solution. Excluded from dominant society, Mexican-Americans have long depended upon an intracultural reciprocity called *mutualismo.* For material needs, one may turn to family or a *tanda* (a kind of rotating credit union). For emotional support, one turns to a family member, a friend, or clergyperson who is respected and who has connections throughout the community, but especially one who enjoys *confianza*. Being of the same community as well as being a personal confidant, this person both shares the same cultural framework, and is a respected source of advice, direction, or prayer. This person may also belong to a *tejido*, an informal group composed of family and fictive kin who help each other in times of need. This interdependency respects the dignity and responsibility of each person. Hence it ascribes neither to a false sense of individualism nor to a practical atheism. That is so because of a deep bonding and coresponsibility, as well as a belief in the omnipresence of a beneficient God. It is this kind of grassroots folk-therapy of family, friends, and faith that is the natural first step for the Mexican-American, rather than the accredited professional to whom an Anglo would normally turn.

Second, there also exists a "cultural chasm" between most conventional treatments and this identified patient. That is so because this treatment is based on paradigms from the dominant population that are not shared by nondominant cultures. The chasm is created both by its high cost and by the parallel poverty (complicated by a lack of insurance or government aid) typical of minority communities. To cross this chasm, one may have to negotiate its inconvenient location, the obstruction of variant languages and belief systems, and sometimes the unscalable cliff of racism.[9] And even in the rare instances when such treatment has been helpful, it may set up an unhealthy dependence. Individually, the client is dependent upon a therapist. Socially, this treatment facility or program is dependent upon forces outside of the Mexican-American community, e.g. government funding. Obviously, conventional treatment is not adequate, and there is a consequent high utilization of the alternative folk therapy, or *mutualismo*, mentioned above.

Alcoholics Anonymous: Essential and Potential

If conventional professional treatment is not adequate, what about the avowed nonprofessional approach of A.A.? Unlike conventional treatment, A.A. is extremely inexpensive. This means that it is within the economic means of the community (it is wholly dependent on members' donations) and is always answerable to that community. Since A.A. meets in the neighborhood, transportation is usually no problem. And when it is made up of persons from that neighborhood, e.g. other Mexican-Americans, language and belief systems are not obstacles, but entrees for the patient identified above. Moreover, A.A. does not ignore the already existing pattern of folk therapy in a community—rather, it capitalizes on it. Parallels to the alternate support system (*mutualismo*) are apparent at first perusal. A.A., like the Mexican *mutualismo*, is based on reciprocal help among adherents, a strong sense of community, a relationship to a Higher Power, and a belief in the dignity and responsibility of the individual. A.A. sets up neither a dependence between client and patient (reciprocity means *all* are recovering alcoholics and therefore equals), nor dependence on outside financing. Government funding, when available, may be more wisely spent in the areas of research and education.

Yet can this program, developed in Akron, Ohio, in 1935 by middle-class, Protestant Anglos, help the low-bottom Mexican-American of today?[10] At this point in the investigation (VER) the search may be only twofold: first looking at the procedural structure (i.e., the formal organization) of A.A., and then examining its substance (its essential ideology).

The structure of A.A. has been described as "benign anarchy." It was intentionally created with as little formal structure as possible. It levies no dues, keeps few records, and requires nothing except the desire to not drink. Anytime two or more persons with this desire decide to meet at regular times, they may call themselves A.A. so long as they do not, as a group, affiliate themselves with other causes. Hence, procedurally, for example, A.A. cannot require anyone to ascribe to any particular religion. In fact, members of A.A. pointedly and emphatically refuse to embrace or reject any denomination, or even any set definition for the Higher Power.[11] Each local group is completely autonomous (for instance in the language used and in the setting and structure of the meeting) except in what effects other groups or A.A. as a whole. For these matters, a General Service Board has been created, but it does not legislate.[12] The only and ultimate authority is God. Therefore, one must conclude that procedurally A.A. is open to any alcoholic regardless of religion, class, gender, or ethnicity.[13]

This flexibility is the reason for the phenomenal foreign growth of A.A. Countries other than the United States now dominate both the current membership and projected expansion.[14] This growth is true of Latin America in general and of Mexico in particular.[15] Spanish was the first non-English language in which A.A. literature was translated, and now virtually all A.A. literature is available in this language. The first Spanish-speaking person joined A.A. in 1940, and he soon translated the Big Book.[16] Now the related groups of Alanon and Alateen also operate in Spanish. Furthermore, while professionals (Anglo and Hispanic alike) continue to doubt the efficacy of A.A., the common people do not. Surveys show that an overwhelming majority of both Mexicans and Mexican-Americans recommend A.A. as a treatment for drinking problems.[17]

A.A. is operating in a Latino setting, specifically among Mexican-Americans. But does it do so in a way respectful of this culture, i.e. is its ideology becoming inculturated, or is it only being translated? Again, in this chapter I am only making preliminary observations; however, I can answer four common criticisms of A.A.

First, the criticism that the ideology of A.A. is effective only with the middle class. The World Health Organization has found A.A. successful among the poor in many Third World countries. A different U.S. study shows that what is important for successful affiliation with A.A. is a certain social stability that, while often associated with the middle class, is in no way limited to it. This same study describes succinctly the essential characteristics of an A.A. member. Parallels with the profile of the identified patient are obvious:

> . . . . the successful A.A. affiliate is characterized by affiliative- and group-dependency needs, a proneness to guilt, considerable experience with social processes which have labeled him as deviant, and relative physical stability at the time of entrance into treatment.[18]

The identified Mexican-American patient is group-oriented, yet marginated from this group because of deviant drinking.[19] However, he is not usually a skid-row derelict, but rather enjoys a certain physical stability provided by his immediate family.[20]

Therefore, it would seem that the essential sociopsychological predispositions for successful A.A. affiliation are not dependent on middle-class values, nor would the identified Mexican-American alcoholic be excluded.

The second and third criticisms, however, are somewhat more problematic. Addressing them will be one of the important roles of the pastoral agent.

First is the acceptance of alcoholism as a disease. Although most Mexican-Americans agree with this principle, alcoholism is still commonly associated with shame and moral weakness. However, this same ambivalence is rampant also in Anglo society. Second is the A.A. insistence that the recovering alcoholic make amends to those he has offended. Although this is difficult for anyone (even with the help of a sponsor and/or confessor), some assert that it presents special difficulties for that Mexican-American male who recognizes the social/moral claims of no one but his father and his God. One must remember, however, the desperate nature of the true alcoholic. Someone who has already lost all respect and honor, and who faces physical and emotional ruin, may well be convinced to follow even this difficult step.[21] As the saying goes: "Nadie está perdido si se tiene el valor de proclamar que todo está perdido y que hay que empezar de nuevo." That is, "No one is truly lost if they have the courage to proclaim that all is lost, and they need to begin over again."

In sum, there are neither procedural nor substantive reasons why A.A. cannot be inculturated as an effective treatment modality for the Mexican-American alcoholic.[22] When A.A. is faithful to its essential and its potential, it is open to all:

> Whenever, wherever, one alcoholic meets another alcoholic and sees in that person first and foremost *not* that he or she is male or female, or black or white, or Baptist or Catholic or Jew, or gay or straight, or *whatever*, but sees rather another alcoholic to whom he or she *must* reach out for the sake of his or her own sobriety—so long, in other words, as one alcoholic recognizes in another alcoholic first and foremost that he or she *is* alcoholic and that therefore *both* of them need each other—there will be not only *an* Alcoholics Anonymous, but there will be *the* Alcoholics Anonymous that you and I love so much and respect so deeply.[23]

Although A.A. is not the only treatment effective for this population, it is the only treatment that is not financially dependent on the dominant society. It also draws almost exclusively on the natural support system *(mutualismo)* extant in this culture. This is why A.A. has been called an "indigenous folk therapy." When A.A. is inculturated, there exists no chasm between it and the people, because the sponsors (folk therapists) *are* the relatives, *padrinos,* and *carnales* to whom people naturally turn in times of need. The recovering alcoholic sponsor is already a part of this alternative utilization network; that person's authority is based not on academic accreditation but on the cultural credit given to one who is like the drinking alcoholic in all things except sobriety.[24] If deeply rooted in a culture, A.A. is an effective, inexpensive, and accessible indigenous support system that soon becomes economically self-supporting and personally empowering. The community no longer looks for a panacea outside itself; rather, it capitalizes on the inner, natural resources too often neglected both by foreign professionals and by the "local notables" within the community.

The lack of involvement of these "local notables," (i.e. indigenous, influential, often professional persons) is an important reason why A.A. is not nearly as widespread among Mexican-Americans as among either Anglos or other Latinos.[25] There are two sides to this noncooperation, but a single justification. Many Mexican-American professionals and A.A. "old-timers" share an experiential epistemology, i.e. the belief that new data ought not be considered independently with regard only to scientific rules of evidence and reasoning, but rather should be examined on the basis of preexisting concepts or experience.[26] For Mexican-American professionals, this preexisting concept is their culture; therefore, they may prematurely dismiss A.A. because it began outside their culture. The preexisting concept for A.A. "old-timers" is a set of beliefs about alcoholism and recovery; therefore, they may prematurely discount unfamiliar considerations such as the importance of inculturation or new professional insights. Breaking down this dual dogmatism, and addressing alcoholism as a disease with its consequent effect on relationships (the two problematic criticisms mentioned above), is the role of the pastoral agent.[27]

Before moving on to the specific role of the pastoral agent, a last criticism must be met, i.e. that the ideology of A.A. is not

compatible with the majority faith of Mexican-Americans. Certainly on the level of official Catholic doctrine no conflict exists.[28]
Moreover, the Mexican-American's *religiosidad* would seem to
make him especially sympathetic to certain A.A. essentials, such
as: (1) a Higher Power—*Dios*—is the True and Ultimate locus of
control in life; (2) the human is a social, spiritual, and moral
being; and (3) as one has been helped, so one must help others
(mutualismo).[29] However, when we deal with this core concept of
change, or conversion, which is central to A.A. (and which is also
central to a change in the perception of alcoholism as a disease,
and the willingness to make personal amends), we must take a
much more serious look at this religiosity, or popular spirituality.
This is precisely the task of the following chapters.

Role of the Pastoral Agent

The leaven of this change, or conversion, is the pastoral agent.
Any such minister serving the Mexican-American community is
or ought to be aware that there is a fatal disease that afflicts an
identifiable portion of the Church, and that is causing physical,
moral, and spiritual harm to the Body of Christ. Current treatment has not proved helpful in arresting this insidious epidemic.
A.A. takes a spiritual (and arguably Biblical) approach to treatment, insisting on the responsibility and concomitant empowering of the identified patient. Unlike other treatments that
operate on client-professional dependency, and that are financially controlled by persons outside the community, A.A. can be
inculturated at the root of the natural healing network of Mexican
mutualismo, becoming an indigenous, inexpensive, available, and
effective folk therapy. If the pastoral agent sees his or her role as
building up the Body of Christ, and would cooperate in the healing ministry of Jesus, the spiritual program of A.A., and its idea
of a necessary "spiritual awakening," is eminently worthy of attention.

Moreover, the pastoral agent holds a unique role in this community for two reasons. First, each recognized minister in the
Church holds an entree into this community because of the people's respect for the things of God. An effective pastoral agent is
already an accepted person of *confianza*, one to whom those in

need naturally turn. Therefore, she or he can be a catalyst between A.A. and the people, reframing their functional belief system in a way that makes A.A. appear as it is, a renewed *mutualismo* that will help their alcoholic brothers. Second, the pastoral agent can act as a broker between Mexican-American professionals and A.A. "old timers." Because the agent is a professional, she or he can speak as a peer to other Mexican-American professionals. And because the agent is a person of God, she or he can exhibit a sympathy to the spiritual program of A.A. "old timers." This is a unique role in that it can bring about cooperation from what often has been competition. Therefore, the role of the pastoral agent in inculturating A.A. is twofold: catalyst and cultural broker. As a cultural broker, his or her role is to:

> [create] linkages between self-help groups and the wider structures of society. . . . [A mediator who] can help to articulate reciprocal relations . . . across organizations . . . contribut[ing] to the implementation of exchange between groups with separate belief systems and problem-solving traditions, such as professionals and members of self-help groups.[30]

In this role, the pastoral agent is working to understand and network with other professionals in the local community, and to convince them that A.A. is more than their preconceptions of it. By presenting at one and the same time *only* the necessary essential, but also the powerful potential of A.A., she or he attempts to create an alliance with other professionals, not to dominate but rather to inculturate A.A. While respecting the self-help (*mutualismo*) concept, possible areas of cooperation and alliance can be explored. These may include such topics of interest to professionals as advocacy and education. Although A.A. as a group does not broach these issues, it can inspire a cohort who, under separate auspices, can do this very important work. One can give many examples of how A.A. has, with the cooperation of local notables, worked not in competition, but rather as an essential cooperative component in a multifaceted approach to Mexican-American alcoholism.[31] With the understanding and support of local professionals, A.A. can be inculturated, resulting both in great success for the treatment of the "low-bottom" male, and in motivating the community to address related aspects of this epidemic. Regarding professionals, then, the role of the pastoral agent can be one of cultural broker, an articulate liaison who negotiates alliances between professionals and nonprofessionals (*mutualistas*), making their different experiences relevant to each other.

A catalyst is a substance that, when added to two dormant elements, causes them to interact. A pastoral agent can be a catalyst for *confianza* between the Mexican-American people and A.A., awakening in these distinct elements their fundamental similarities. A key similarity to be explored in the next two chapters is the dynamics of conversion.

The pastoral agent can work directly with the people, placing them in interaction with A.A. by: (1) distributing A.A. literature; (2) encouraging attendance at A.A. open meetings; (3) inviting A.A. members to speak at Church functions; (4) preaching and teaching on alcoholism as a disease, rather than as a moral weakness; (5) helping the recovering alcoholic and his family heal those relationships harmed by the disease, and the related phenomenon of codependency; (6) being a resource to A.A. as a spiritual companion, confessor or speaker; (7) helping in the holistic integration of the deviant back into the community; and (8) using A.A. for intervention, i.e. asking A.A. members to visit and talk to problem drinkers. Some further explanation of numbers four and five are necessary. Note that both deal with reframing, changing, or conversion, which A.A. calls a "spiritual awakening."

There exists in the Mexican-American community some ambiguity about the disease concept of alcoholism. While most admit believing in this concept, they still associate it with moral weakness. To challenge these misconceptions, the preparation of the pastoral agent will be important, as perhaps it will be for professional speakers also. But most convincing will be recovering alcoholics themselves, who can tell the people about their struggle, and how their victory depended not on inner, moral strength but rather on a conversion ("spiritual awakening") to the things of God. This will be a believable testimonial especially if the person's life and recovery are already well-known in the community. Another convincing argument is to point out the inconsistency between disease and weakness. After all, we do not ascribe moral weakness to other diseases, like cancer and diabetes. If alcoholism is a disease, it cannot also be a sin. It is an embarrassment, but not a moral weakness.

Similarly, there is an inconsistency in the recovering alcoholic who has given his will over to God (conversion) but refuses to follow God's law, to make amends to the persons the alcoholic has harmed. The Mexican-American male may not admit to a moral claim from his wife or children, but he may be convinced that God, to whom he does owe obedience, demands these amends. Moreover, he will acknowledge his responsibility as provider and role model—sufficient amends may be simply becoming the best husband and father he can. These issues strike at the heart of the A.A. phenomenon of conversion. Because of its centrality to A.A. and the Christian life, and the life of the Mexican-American and the pastoral agent ministering to him, the topic of conversion in this population will be broached at length in the next chapter.

Both by reframing this functional belief system and by making the people more sensitive to the disease concept of alcoholism, the pastoral agent is preparing the culture to draw on its own best intuition in order to accept the wisdom of A.A.

In complementary fashion, the pastoral agent is also working directly with A.A. to insure its sensitivity to the culture by (1) identifying bilingual, bicultural A.A. members and asking them to form a group of Mexican-Americans; (2) encouraging A.A. not to confuse essentials with accidentals (e.g., the Higher Power can be a patron saint or *La Virgen,* and A.A. literature can be adapted to barrio Spanish); (3) offering an inviting place for their meetings; (4) encouraging experimentation with new techniques and slogans;[32] and (5) constantly challenging sponsors to be faithful both to the essentials of A.A. and the integrity of the Mexican-American culture.[33]

As cultural broker and as catalyst the pastoral agent has a unique role to play because, precisely as an agent of *this* Church, she or he can understand and relate to both the spiritual essentials of A.A. and the cultural reality of the Mexican-American community. As both an accepted member of the *mutualismo* and a peer of professionals, she or he can mediate between the two. The agent's role is an art and a ministry requiring both an appreciation of ancient and venerated traditions, and an openness to adapting new and effective methods in the service of the Reign of God.

> Todo . . . discípulo del Reino de los Cielos se parece a un padre de familia que, de sus reservas, va sacando cosas nuevas y cosas antiguas.[34]

2

A Return to the Roots: Conversion and the Culture of the Mexican-Descent Catholic

In the previous chapter I identified a key concept in the understanding of Alcoholics Anonymous, and therefore in its inculturation, as conversion. By conversion I mean a

> . . . radical reorientation of one's desires, thought processes, and actions [on both a conscious and unconscious level] . . . requir[ing] a fundamental shift in the symbols and images that inform . . . decision making.[1]

A careful inculturation of A.A. must begin with an understanding of conversion from inside the Mexican-descent, Catholic milieu, and then compare that understanding with how conversion is experienced and encouraged among A.A. members. This first task is the work of the present chapter.

Although I am painfully aware that we urgently need a multidimensional, diachronic analysis of the various Hispanic spiritualities that enrich the Catholic experience in the United States,[2] this is beyond the scope of a single chapter. My aim is much more modest, and consists of three parts: 1) the parameters of the study; 2) an account of three rites; and 3) a description of conversion.

Parameters of the Study

As a priest and a Franciscan, I am concerned specifically with the religious aspects of conversion, with particular attention to the role of culture. Because the United States Catholic Church is, and always has been, composed of many different cultures, any attempt to analyze conversion in this local church must deal with these unique cultural manifestations. Although tomes have been written about religious conversion, very few treat cultural considerations, and virtually nothing has been written about the experience of conversion among Hispanics.[3]

The specific population I am considering is the Catholic, Mexican-descent community in the United States. Further specification of this heterogenous group is difficult. However, since I am presuming a role for popular spirituality, one can assume a certain traditionalism. Nevertheless, it is important to remember that this society is diverse and changeable. Different segments of this group are at different points in acculturation to U.S. society. Some date their ancestry from before Jamestown, others arrived today. They are among themselves a racial, social, linguistic, economic, and political mixture in constant flux.[4] In order to make this study manageable, I have limited myself to a largely synchronic snapshot of the present Mexican-descent Catholic practices of popular spirituality. The historical origins of this spirituality have been explored, and future projections are tenuous. Hence, while ignoring neither the past nor the future, I concentrate on what is the present reality.

The typology of the study is descriptive, not analytic. It deals with the intratraditional intensification aspect of conversion, that is, how a Mexican-descent Catholic becomes recommitted to his or her own faith through a retrieval of its symbol system.[5]

I shall use a heuristic and holistic framework to describe how a Mexican-descent Catholic is revitalized (converted) through his or her experience of popular spirituality.[6] This framework is largely drawn from the work of Lewis Rambo, both because of the paucity of specifically U.S. Hispanic frameworks, and because I see an affinity between his sensitivity to culture and the model of U.S. Hispanic conversion offered by Orlando Costas, which I use in the conclusion of this chapter.

I choose popular spirituality as the source for this study because it is the most pristine expression of the uniqueness of Mexican-descent spirituality.[7] Popular spirituality is widely accepted now as the locus of any attempt to reach into the peculiarity of the Hispanic worlds.

The context of the study is threefold: 1) macrocontext, or world environment; 2) microcontext, or the personal world of the individual; and 3) mesocontext, or those aspects that mediate between the macrocontext and microcontext.[8] The macrocontext of this population is the experience of *mestizaje*, i.e. the birth of a new culture from the fusion of Native-American, African-American, and Spanish peoples.[9] The microcontext is popular spirituality, i.e. the domestic religious experience of the people, which is neither controlled by the clergy nor dependent on formal Church structures. Most authors accept the basic definition of popular spirituality offered at *Puebla:*

> . . . the whole context of underlying belief rooted in God, the basic attitudes that flow from these beliefs, and the expressions that manifest them. It is the form of cultural life that religion takes . . . [as] an expression of the Catholic Faith.[10]

The mesocontext is the formal Church structure, i.e. the clergy, parish, Sacraments, and Creed. The mediation by the mesocontext between the micro- and macrocontexts is not necessarily a conflictual one, although this is often the case.[11] Indeed, the diminution of popular spirituality is often due to the control or repression of it by official church structures, or to the access to modernity and secularity mediated through these structures.

As the source of this study is the popular spirituality of the Mexican-descent Catholic in the United States, it will deal specifically with those rites that are both universal within this population, and unique to it. These rites of passage, incorporation, and revitalization are not just devotional anachronisms, but the *sensus fidei* through which one can detect and describe a compelling and comprehensive world view.[12] A description of conversion as here defined will be a delineation of how a member of this population might experience a recommitment to this world view through a retrieval of the symbols (contained in these rites) of his or her own spirituality precisely to give new order, purpose, and meaning to his or her life.

It is my hope that this tentative, synchronic description will contribute to that eventual multidimensional, diachronic analysis sorely needed.

In order to explain the experience of Mexican-descent, Catholic popular spirituality in context, I have borrowed and adapted several diagrams from other authors who are also concerned with culture and conversion, and whose theoretical foundations can

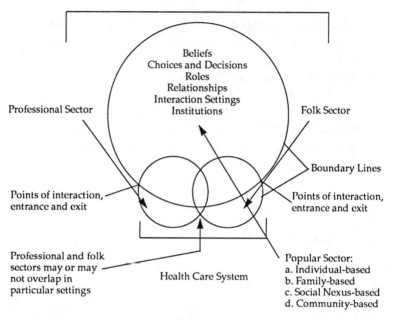

Figure 1.

be adapted to the U.S. Hispanic context. For instance, figure 1 is taken from Arthur Kleinman's *Patients and Healers in the Context of Culture*. It can be adapted to provide a good, graphic description of the Mexican-descent spiritual universe. For example, the folk sector ("nonprofessional, semisacred specialist") corresponds to the experience of *curanderismo*.[13] However, since the popular sector, specifically popular spirituality, is the source of my study, I shall not deal with the folk sector as such. I consider the professional sector to be official Church structures. All of this is set within the macrocontext of a dominant society and its world view.

The problem with Kleinman's construct is that each sphere is bounded, i.e. it has clear, inviolate boundaries that contain definite, uniform, and limited essential characteristics. This is a correct construct for the professional sphere, but the popular sphere is a centered, unbounded set (see figure 2). A centered set is "created by defining the center and the relationship of things to that center." Therefore, it is dynamic because the boundary is not immutable, but is defined by one's relationship to the center.[14] A more appropriate model for the Mexican-descent,

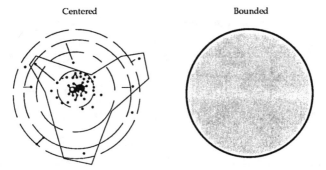

Centered   Bounded

Figure 2. Bounded and Centered Sets.

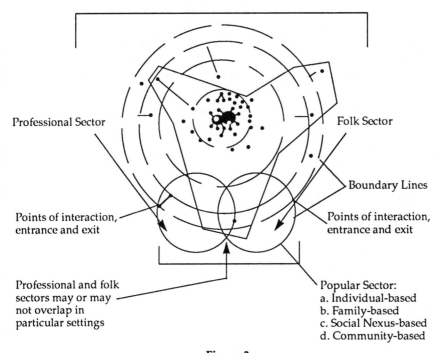

Professional Sector

Folk Sector

Boundary Lines

Points of interaction, entrance and exit

Points of interaction, entrance and exit

Professional and folk sectors may or may not overlap in particular settings

Popular Sector:
a. Individual-based
b. Family-based
c. Social Nexus-based
d. Community-based

Figure 3.

Catholic spiritual universe in context, then, is shown in figure 3. The dots with lines on the centered set can be conceived as individuals either moving closer to or farther from the center. The sphere of popular spirituality is a centered set, defined by one's relationship to the Divine, and it is this relationship that effects how one interconnects with other individuals and with institutions.

The Divine is the Godhead, and closest to It are Jesus and
Mary. Closest to them are the angels and saints. All of these
personages are considered close enough to the Divinity to have
influence over It, and yet close enough to humanity to have com-
passion on us. The traditional, Mexican-descent, Catholic culture
defines itself, and both prescribes and proscribes behavior, according to the Divine. One always exists in relationship to the
Divine, no matter the contextual constraints, and one has some
control over one's relationship to the Divine, who always awaits
one's return and ultimately, in death if not in life, will have Its
way with us. The Godhead is demanding and just, and therefore
it is to one's benefit to enlist the aid of the angels and saints (and
especially Mary) in the quest to receive aid and forgiveness from
It. This relationship to the angels and saints, however, is mutual—
they intercede for us and we honor them. It sounds mechanical
and selfish, but actually it closely parallels the workings of the
Mexican-descent extended family, and the hierarchy and mutuality therein. Far from being mechanical or selfish, this relationship
is perceived as balanced and nurturing. However, my study will
only try to describe the *ethos* of this belief system; it will not
attempt an analysis of its *pathos*.[15]

The object of this study, then, is to describe the experience of
an individual in this culture who begins to move toward the Divine, to become "centered." We see in figure three that the individual is always dynamic and multifaceted, in relation to several
spheres of influence. What is the change that overcomes an individual and motivates her or him towards the center of the microcontext (popular spirituality)? This requires a closer look at the
individual and her or his ritual behavior (microcontext) in relation
to the macro- and mesocontexts.

Remember that the center of the universe for this person is not
the individual, but the Divine (powers). How she or he relates to
the macrocontext (dominant society) is dependent and expressed
by his or her world view (i.e., metaphysical and cosmological
beliefs). A strong, independent world view, for instance, can resist
the philosophical and religious domination of the macrocontext
even when the person is not critically conscious of this inner
strength. How the individual relates to the microcontext and mesocontext are dependent upon and expressed by his or her formal
(expressive, ritualistic) behavior. The formal behaviors I will dis-

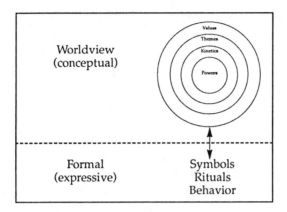

Figure 4.

cuss—rites of passage, incorporation, and revitalization—can be ways of retrieving the power of the microcontext (popular spirituality) in concert with, or in opposition to, the mesocontext, or formal church structures. However, there is a mutual influence between world view and formal behavior, an influence that can be conceptualized as: 1) kinetic, or the nature of the Divine in its relationship to the individual and society; 2) themes, or specific kinds of ritualistic behavior (e.g., rites of passage); and 3) values that the culture holds that arise from its kinetics and are expressed in its themes.[16] This mutual influence can be diagramed as shown in figure 4.

In order to describe the retrieval of a world view as expressed in formal behavior (specifically the rituals and themes of popular spirituality), the kinetics and values contained in religious themes within this population must be described. I move now to an examination of three universal but unique religious themes among the Mexican-descent, Catholic population of the United States (i.e., rites of passage, revitalization, and incorporation) drawn from their popular spirituality.

Because this population often experiences official Church structures (while not necessarily opposed to the kinetics of their spirituality) as routinized, bureaucratic, and intolerant of its popular themes and values, I must, in order to avoid cultural chauvinism, delve into their popular spirituality as the source of any depiction of Mexican-descent kinetics and values. To accomplish this analysis I will look at the time and space concepts involved (how the

world is related to the Divine), and the underlying epistemology—what the culture believes are values worth nurturing.

Rite of Passage

The Mexican-descent, Catholic community has a plethora of
religious rites of passage (e.g, *Quinceañera*, the coming-of-age of
a fifteen-year-old girl). However, of these, those that are most
truly popular (not dependent on formal Church structure), universal (common throughout this diverse population), and unique
(differing significantly from the popular spirituality of other
Catholic groups) are the rites of passage concerning death. These
rites are enacted both at the moment of biological death, and
at certain moments when Death itself is celebrated, rather than
individual deaths.

Time in death rituals is not linear, nor truly cyclical; it is relational. One celebrates death at the moment of biological death,
on the anniversary of the death of related persons and on the
Day of the Dead. These last two appear to be cyclical celebrations,
but actually they, too, are based on relationships. Anniversaries
are celebrated based on one's relationship to the deceased, and
the Day of the Dead is celebrated (1) Because the dead choose to
return this day because of our relationship to them (and the Divine); and (2) because generally only the souls of those to whom
one was related are domestically remembered.

A strong belief in the afterlife is based on this relational understanding of time: God does not wish our destruction, therefore
death is not an end to life, but only a change. This is why Death
is not denied, but is personified.[17]

Time is also considered relational in the sense that the amount
of time we have on earth depends on the Divine, upon which
our life and death depend. Thus, death is seen not as an end to
existence, but as a door to a different life. It is our relationship to
time (ultimately through the eternal God) that influences all our
other relationships, i.e. how we treat others and expect them to
treat us. People judge themselves and others not so much by
their ability or inability to properly conceive of God and others
(orthodoxy), but rather on their actual conduct towards God and

others (orthopraxis). If one has struggled to be good in this life, one (and one's family) can count on God's goodness in the next.

> Roman Catholicism has provided a fundamental set of beliefs and has also established guidelines for appropriate and inappropriate behavior . . . anxiety surrounding death [therefore], the individual's or another's, is ideally reduced through the belief that the person will experience . . . atonement and release.[18]

Now, this is not fatalism, that is, the passive acceptance of an immutable pattern predetermined by God. Rather, it is a belief in destiny, a supernatural goal desired by God for all. Since all of Divinity essentially occupies the same time and space as humanity, the saints and other deceased are all related to us and to God on a continuum oriented toward the Godhead. Even death cannot sever this relationship, since God is the God of Time and therefore of Death. Our relationship to the Godhead distinguishes us from the deceased (and among them the saints). They are closer to It than we are; therefore we need and invoke their intercession, for the agreed destiny of all human beings is, or ought to be, eventual communion with the Divinity.[19]

It is precisely their relationship to the deceased in space and time that effects grief and bereavement. As this relationship cannot be fundamentally altered even by death, they can still have an effect on the destiny of the deceased through prayer and penance, just as the deceased can affect the living by interceding with the Godhead. As death, then, is highly personal and relational, so is time, which is profoundly affected by relationships.[20]

That is why linear time, or punctuality, is of less importance: The correctness of time is not judged impersonally by a clock, but rather personally, when all relationships are present and accounted for. This ultimate dependence of Time on God is expressed through numerous sayings: "If God so wills," "If God grants it," "God first." While these sayings can be formulaic, and socially acceptable ways of avoiding conflict, the common wisdom expressed is that ultimately God is Destiny, i.e. our source and our goal.

Indeed, time is so relational that death not only does not sever bonds between people, it creates new ones. While biological bonds with the deceased are broken, psychosocial and religious bonds are strengthened. Their survivors are linked to them by stories, photographs, Masses and prayers, candles, visits to the grave, and other ways the living perpetuate the memory of their departed. The dead also maintain the bond—by intercession, visitations, or advice (often in dreams). Moreover, death rites strengthen bonds among the living. Families scattered by years and miles will suffer great hardships to prepare and participate in the funeral of a relative. Each individual, from eldest to youngest, has a role and relationships to maintain that are strongly reinforced during death rites.[21]

The celebration of the Days of the Dead (31 October–2 November) emphasizes the belief in a spirit filled universe, a world where there are no impregnable boundaries between spirit and matter, life and afterlife. This celebration of Death touches the most mundane places and moments of both public and private affairs.[22] People dance and joke with Death, men exhibit their bravery in confronting death, women show their nurturing by preparing for the return of the dead, children demonstrate their innocence by eating candy skulls and ritually destroying Death. Death is so much a part of life that, like a close friend, it can at once be teased and respected.[23] Every sense is involved in the feast—incense burns, food is eaten, candles are lighted, bells are rung, decorations are crafted. All of this requires family and community cooperation (both from living and deceased members, blood relatives and fictive kin) and occasions intense social activity.[24]

The kinetics, then, of the rites of death are essentially incarnational: Divinity dwells with us, shares our time and space, is the source and goal of our destiny. The Godhead, though just and demanding, is good, and does not desire our destruction. These rites, then, tend to have a strong centripetal force: Death is not denied, but celebrated, and social relationships (roles) and the relationship to Divinity are ritually reinforced. To encounter God, one need not reject this culture, but rather allow its *ethos*, as expressed in this rite of passage, to draw one toward the world view therein expressed: A good and just God is the source and goal of humanity, dwells with humanity, and neither sin nor death can break this covenant. Mexican-descent Catholics, by being true to themselves and their culture, are true to the Christian God.

The theme I am considering is a rite of passage, i.e. rite of death. The kinetics involved are incarnational and essentially Christian. What values are encoded in this rite? I identify three essential and complex ones.

1) *Respeto y Vergüenza:* the foundation of both the hierarchy and mutality of the extended family, and of its position on the continuum oriented towards the Godhead.
2) The simultaneous experience of the world as both divinely ordained, but not rigidly ordered.
3) The belief that suffering (especially of the poor and humble) is redemptive and liberating.

Since these values are encountered in the other two rites I will consider, a further elaboration of each is needed.

The Mexican-descent culture has been described as a shame culture (as opposed to a guilt culture). One's behavior is pre-scribed and proscribed not by an individual's sense of personal guilt, but rather by the shame *(vergüenza)* or respect *(respeto)* such behavior will bring to the family. What one must or must not do to avoid shame and to engender respect is conditioned by one's gender, status, and age.[25] One's role and therefore one's acceptable behavior is fairly well understood and accepted by all. Thus, the cultural *ethos* for the adult male is that he is a good provider, is strict, is responsible, loyal, dependable, modest, helpful, happy, and protective. The adult female's role is to nurture and raise children, provide for domestic comfort and harmony, and be re-served and pious, emotional but respectful. Children are social-ized into these roles, and the diminishing capacities of the elderly are mitigated by these same roles, because one is judged by who one is rather than by what one produces. Ideally, each role is mutually beneficial to the whole, and harmoniously balanced. One who fulfills these roles is considered good and worthy of respect. One who egregiously violates them is considered a shameless member of a shameless family.[26]

A "good" funeral or other death rite, then, is one in which these roles are revitalized. The women pray and prepare food, the men make the economic sacrifices necessary and do the hard labor, the elderly speak reverently of the deceased and the past, children are socialized, and fictive kin and friends all help in the preparations and consolation. Each has his or her own way, prescribed and proscribed by shame and respect, to honor the dead and reanimate bonds with the living, and in so doing participate in turning the whole family and community towards the center of their existence, the Divine. This hierarchy and mutuality within the extended family is experienced also with the Divinity, especially in these moments, through the deceased. It is presumed that if one maintains a respectful relationship to the deceased (fulfills one's role) she or he therefore will respond by signs on earth and help from heaven. Respect and shame, then, are the foundation for the mutuality and hierarchy of relationships both horizontally (among the living), and vertically (between the living and the dead). By fulfilling the role of mourner according to his or her role, a "good" person sees that both humanity and Divinity will honor and aid the beloved deceased.

Reality is ordained by Divinity: God creates and governs all, and wills that humans return to God. The foolish person defies God by trying to control time and space. The good person accepts the mastery of God, and endeavors to live in harmony with the environment instead of dominating it.[27] This is not fatalism, that is, a universe so immutably ordered that human freedom has no role. Humans have the freedom to be foolish, but that freedom cannot change destiny—humanity is created by and for God. This, too, is reflected in the family: Although roles are ordained, they are not rigidly ordered. Men's articlerical attitudes, women's gossip, and children's competition, all normally recognized and accepted behaviors, are mitigated at death by the necessity to honor the dead with the proper familial harmony and religious observances. The universe is ordained, but it is a centered set, not ordered and defined in defiance of the ultimate value: the relationships to the Divine and among the community.[28]

The rites of popular spirituality are anti-elitist and historically, if not actually, are the product of what the Old Testament prophets called the "remnant of society." For the remnant of society, suffering is as indubitable as death. Ada María Isasi-Díaz correctly identifies Hispanics as a contemporary remnant community.[29] However, they do not view this as a way of justifying themselves through sacrifice, nor do they see sacrifice primarily as deferred gratification. Rather, sacrifice, penance, and suffering is their way of uniting themselves to Divinity, especially through the Crucified Christ and the Sorrowful Mother. Sanctity in this view is not a recompense earned through suffering, but suffering is an essential part of centering, or returning to Divinity. Suffering is redemptive because it is believed that, since God is incarnate, by sharing in the suffering of the Divine, one will share also in Its sanctity.[30]

However, this is not a religion of resignation: Even its apparent passivity is really passive aggression, sometimes the safest form of protest for the oppressed.[31] The very existence of this popular spirituality after over 140 years of oppression from the macrocontext and at best benign neglect from the mesocontext, speaks of its important role as a symbolic strategy for survival.[32] It is precisely the rites of popular spirituality that have maintained the cohesive world view and cultural identity of this people, and as such contains the seed of its liberation. The secular world and official Church have often looked upon this peculiar microcontext with paternalism or disdain: They should look on it with awe, because it has managed for centuries to silently subvert their efforts at imperialism.[33] It is the strong centripetal force of the death rites, coming as they do at moments of crisis, that tends to reinforce the identity of the community, assures them that there is meaning in their suffering, and socializes the next generation into this meaning-making milieu.[34]

Rite of Revitalization

Of the three kinds of rites considered, the rites of revitalization are perhaps the least unique. While there are some peculiarly Mexican-descent elements to them, at least in outward form they resemble similar rites throughout the Catholic world. I am speaking of the feasts and pilgrimages associated with Mary, the saints, and angels. These are rites of revitalization because they revitalize a relationship to the holy patron involved, and they revive human bonds because these rites are familial or communal.

The sphere of popular spirituality reveres many saints, some officially canonized and some not. It is not uncommon that someone who died unjustly, or some charismatic or heroic person, is revered as a saint after death.[35] Curiously, these popularly recognized saints share much in common with the majority of canonized saints: 1) they were so completely dedicated to serving the people that they were uninterested in wealth, family, or personal ambition—these characteristics parallel the religious vows of poverty, chastity, and obedience; 2) they were and are considered privileged channels to the Divine and, as in the case of canonized saints, this is an accepted deviation from the usual nominal public role of males in spirituality; and 3) each popular saint is considered a traditional innovator, i.e. someone who maintained but adapted popular spirituality to specific circumstances.[36] It seems, then, that although the popular process of naming someone a saint is firmly within the microcontext, the criteria for this evaluation are heavily influenced by the mesocontext. The role of popular and canonized saints, both in life and after death, is the defense, sometimes through innovation, of the microcontext in the face of the overwhelming influence of the macrocontext.

The context of time in the rites of revitalization appears to be cyclical, i.e. a regularly occurring event measured by the seasons. Although this tends to be more the case in rural settings, time is still thought of as relational. After all, even in rural settings the celebration of particular saints is not universal, but rather based on which saint is considered the patron of a particular locale. Although the feast is celebrated on the same day each year, its existence is based on a relationship and not on a universally recognized calendar. Moreover, urban popular spirituality quite readily moves the feasts to the closest weekend in order to celebrate without the constraints of employment.[39] Obviously, the feast is maintained because of a relational concept of time. It is moved because a cyclical date is considered convenient but not essential. Even in rural areas, a crisis can force the feast to be celebrated on another day, but can never be an excuse not to celebrate the relationship at all. Certain feast days then are considered sanctified, but this is due to a relationship to a patron saint, not just a recurrent natural cycle.

This is precisely what distinguishes popular feasts from officially liturgical ones. Church structure insists that liturgical feasts are cyclical and operate an elaborate calendar to coordinate these official feasts. While some official feasts are also popular, the popular conception is based much more on a relational appreciation of time than a cyclical one.[38]

Sacred space is commonplace in this culture. While these are no strict delineations between secular and sacred, certain places are considered especially touched by the Divine. Again, some officially recognized places (basilicas) are also popularly approved, but popular spirituality can also consider a space sacred with little or no official Church recognition.

A place of popular devotion may be sanctified by what occurred there. Crosses are erected at the site of recent deaths; caves, rivers, and groves are sanctified by popular myth. Sometimes, promises to saints are kept by erecting outdoor shrines. Most any person, vehicle, or business is graced with at least one holy image. But the most common expression of sacred space in popular spirituality is the *altarcito* (a tiny altar in the home).

A corner of even the humblest home is often dedicated to God through an arrangement of holy images, candles, flowers, souvenirs, and family photos. This is where the cycle of both horizontal (between humans) and vertical (between humans and the Divine) mutuality occurs. Favors are asked of the saints, devout persons intercede for family or friends, glasses of water are left for the deceased, and the images of the saints are implored, punished, or attended, depending on how the personages they represent have responded to human pleas.

It is in this corner of the home that we see the declamatory function of sacred space. It both praises and exhorts the Divine, and evangelizes and socializes the human. Since life is considered a gift, not an investment, nor sacrifice a self-discipline endured for long-term returns, so the Divine is thanked through gifts. Flowers, incense, candles, and memorabilia are all offered as fervent, spontaneous, artistic proclamations of the connection between the human and the Divine. Since all is a gift from the Divine, all must be returned as a gift. Nothing is too secular to offer. On the *altarcitos* and in the feasts, food, money, fireworks, bells, and clothing, everything is given to praise the Divine because everything has been received from the Divine and is made holy by Its presence. Sacred space, then, whether an enormous basilica or a poor altar, is an icon, a figural representation of how Divinity is woven into the ordinary.[39]

The kinetics of these rites are obviously incarnational. God is omnipresent, and as all has been given and sanctified by God's presence, so all must be generously returned to God at those times and places made especially sacred by the explicit representation of God's always-and-everywhere implicit presence. To encounter or return to God, one need not reject but rather more explicitly embrace the *ethos* that God is both the source and goal of humanity, dwells with humanity, and is always present and patiently awaiting human "centering." These rites have a centripetal force; Both in daily life and on certain feasts the implicit relationship to God is made explicit, and the goal and source of human life is experienced as palpably present and universally accepted.

The theme of rites of revitalization mirrors the kinetics of the rites of passage. The values encoded in these rites are also essentially the same.

The values of *respeto* and *vergüenza* as the foundation of both horizontal and vertical mutality and hierarchy is present in these rites. As rites of revitalization, they function not only to reinforce this value, but also allow one who has strayed from the values to be revitalized, i.e. received anew by the community. A family can gain *respeto* by accepting a prominent (and costly) role in the preparation of a feast. Also, a communal judgment of shame can be mitigated by a public act of penance, e.g. walking to a shrine. Honoring the saints through private, daily offerings and through occasional public feasts is a way of both earning and recouping the honor that is the basis of all relationships in this culture.[40]

The world is ordained but not rigidly ordered: There is room both for persistency and change in popular spirituality.[41] Although, as in daily life, there is a hierarchy in the organization of feasts and pilgrimages, there is also mutuality. These rites reinforce the social order by establishing, maintaining, and reminding the population of the ordained nature of the universe. However, principal roles (e.g., *mayordomo*, a kind of important and trusted sacristan) are not hereditary, and even the roles based on sex, age, and status are not so rigid as to admit no exceptions. Witness the fact that popular spirituality accepts a female healer even when this means abandoning her role of homemaker, or a male *rezadero* (prayer leader) even though piety is generally thought to be a feminine trait. Because things are ordained to center life on God, exceptions are made when so doing serves this centering.[42]

Although the privileged position of the poor and humble is most clear in the rite of incorporation, some vestiges are found also in these rites of revitalization. Even though the Mexican-descent population is often divided along socioeconomic lines, feast days in particular tend to integrate the classes. In fact, in some cases the burden imposed on the rich is a means of redistributing the wealth of the community. And for more private ceremonies, the institution of *compadrazgo* (godparenthood) provides a socially acceptable way in which a poorer person can receive the help and support of someone wealthy or influential. In almost any rite of revitalization ". . . socioeconomic integration and interaction between individuals . . . takes place."[43] Moreover, although it has been noted that women are the victims of certain *pathos* in this community, it is rarely mentioned that these particular rites are seen not only as redemptive for the whole community through women's (majority) participation, but they also contain the seeds of the liberation of women. In no other sphere do women hold such power, command such respect, or so freely network without any intrusion by men. Popular spirituality, and these rites of revitalization in particular, are potentially significant sources of power for women in this community.[44]

The values of these rites of revitalization can be summarized as paralleling the values of the rite of passage. *Respeto* and *vergüenza* are the foundation of both the horizontal and vertical hierarchy and mutuality. This hierarchy is ordained by God, but not rigidly controlled by humans, because the goal, like the source, of all relationships is communion with God. It is because God wishes to be in communion with the human that God is incarnated, i.e. present in our time and space but most explicit in privileged moments (rites), places *(altarcitos)*, and persons (the suffering).

Rite of Incorporation

It is no exaggeration to claim that the Mexican mentality was born with the appearance of Our Lady of Guadalupe. Nor is it an exaggeration to claim that Mexican-descent popular spirituality is universally and uniquely (almost literally) stamped with her image. She is what the Ark of the Covenant was to the Ancient Jews: a movable symbol of their identity as particularly chosen by the Divine. I call the devotion to Our Lady of Guadalupe a rite of incorporation because it acts to embody and form these heterogeneous people with a sense of unity, despite differences of gender, age, status, geography, politics, incorporating them into a *pueblo* through a sovereign act of God. It is said that in Mexico, even the atheists believe in Our Lady. "Mejicanidad es Guadalupanismo."[45]

The time concept of this rite is supremely relational. Mary chose to reveal herself to and enter into a relationship with Juan Diego, and through him, with all the Mexican people, especially those who suffer. She not only chose to enter into their time, but did so with consummate respect and love. Because she, a woman of color, like indigenous Mexicans, spoke their language, was clothed in their raiment, and was surrrounded by the sights and sounds they associated with Divinity, she at once entered into and created for them *kairói*.[46] By taking on herself their *mestizaje*, she made both their experience and their existence sacred. The moment she entered their time, she became a timeless symbol of their culture, their faith, and their self-understanding.[47]

Space, too, would never be the same. Not only did Our Lady baptize their holy hill of Tepeyac by her appearance and her church, she left her image in time and space on the *tilma* of Juan Diego. She would be forever present for all in a palpable, portable parable, the proof and promise of her protection. It is because she introduces her adherents into *kairói* time and transcendent space that devotion to her has always been highly adaptable. Revolutionaries praise her as the non-European missionary, peasants implore her as Fertile Mother, and urban travelers carry small images of her touched to the original.[48] One could say that she did not enter into time and space as modernity recognizes it, but rather lifted people into a liminal experience of time and space.[49] It is this corporate experience of liminality that incorporates this heterogeneous population into a social and psychological unity that transcends the constraints of race, class, gender, age, and geography.[50] This is what is celebrated on December 12, or anytime that Our Lady's promise to care for her people is invoked— consolidation as a people because they have been chosen by the Divine to be peculiarly incorporated into It.

Again, the kinetics are unabashedly incarnational (indeed when sublimated to Mexican nationalism they can become kinetics of predilection). Divinity not only shares our time and space, but at the same time lifts us into an experience of transcendent time and space. Represented in Our Lady of Guadalupe, the Divinity is the source of the Mexican-descent people's identity, and the consummate goal of their singularity. This remnant people, the object of continuing conquests, dance, sing, and pray to Our Lady of Guadalupe with abandon. It is the centripetal force of this rite that causes the sense of liminality, that sense of belonging or incorporation that crosses all intracommunal differences. When she became one with them, they became one people. Every time they celebrate their oneness with her, this cultural *ethos* is raised up with her image. Divinity is encountered within this particularity, a people is united precisely through Divinity's dwelling within them, and they with it, making them a people peculiarly God's own.[51]

This theme of incorporation contains, in an even more obvious and compelling way, the same three values discussed above.

The roles of *respeto* and *vergüenza* are celebrated each time the story of Our Lady is recounted. Both Mary and Juan Diego are consummate examples of the proper roles of men and women in society.[52] Mary, the true source of power, convinces Juan to take the active role. He must leave the nurturing ambiance of Tepeyac and confront the hostile world. He is respectful both with her and the bishop, but not passive. He not only shows great tenacity with the bishop, he even tries to orchestrate the apparition when it conflicts with his role of family protector (i.e. caring for his ill uncle). Juan is responsible, loyal, dependable, modest, helpful, happy, and a good provider. He is active and tenacious when confronting a hostile world, never losing either his nobility or his perseverance. Mary, too, shows the *respeto* and *vergüenza* expected of a woman. She is nurturing, reserved, and pious, the creator of a harmonious oasis. She calls Juan her child and asks him to build her a home where she may care for her children. They are ideal types, each recognizing through their *respeto* and *vergüenza* the necessary hierarchy and mutuality of their world. By fulfilling their roles with aplomb, they demonstrate the efficacy of this ethos. Our Lady of Guadalupe is a cultural idiom for both their relationship to God and to each other.[53]

The world must be divinely ordained if the "Mother of the True God" deigns to enter it, but while she respects the role of Divinity, she completely reverses the order imposed by humanity. The Spanish bishop had been ordained to bring God's word to the Mexican people. Mary respects this ordination, but reverses the order of things when she sends Juan as her personal missionary to the officially ordained missioner. The person divinely chosen to witness and the person in need of witness present a complete reversal of the social and ecclesial order. Mary moves easily within this ordained world (e.g., she produces the proof the bishop requested), but she is not above fulfilling the reason behind divine ordination through a change in human order. She uses the dress, manners, tongue, color, and hieroglyphics of those supposedly evangelized to truly evangelize those who thought they were the privileged repositories of the Gospel. The human order can change so that the goal of divine ordination may remain the same.[54]

The value of the suffering of the poor and humble is nowhere clearer or more closely connected with kinetics than in the remembrance rites of Our Lady of Guadalupe. A poor, conquered Indian suffering at the hands of those who claim to speak for the Divine, and who may have brought sickness to his house, is chosen, precisely because of his low station, to be the special ambassador of the Divine. Our Lady tells him that she could have chosen anyone, but she chose him to help her erect a church, a home where she could be a good mother to her suffering children. His appointment will mean suffering to him (indeed, it is termed a penance), but he accepts it as his necessary share in making known the Good News. Besides, our Lady promises to be his help and protection: her strength is enough for him. Like a reed that can be played only when it is empty, Juan places himself in Our Lady's hands, confident that she chose the humble in order to make him great.[55] Yet her appearance was not only personally redemptive but publicly liberating. As Virgil Elizondo writes, the conquest of Mexico was fourfold: 1) political-economic, through the imposition of colonialism; 2) sexual, through the violation of native women; 3) sociopsychological, through racial discrimination; and 4) religious, through the eradication of pagan beliefs and their symbols. Our Lady of Guadalupe's irruption into that time and space began the liberation of the conquered. She became the recognized queen of the political-economic order; no one need follow laws that oppressed her people (as several Mexican governments and United States companies have learned). Her appearance as a native maiden vicariously returned the people's honor and purity to them. When she pleads for a place to listen to the poor, and treats their representative, Juan Diego, as a person, she condemns all social and psychological oppression. And by being both woman and native, she liberates persons from the notion that the Divine is exclusively male or European. Our Lady of Guadalupe introduced a process that is by its nature liberating, and indeed has inspired revolutionaries and reformers from Hidalgo to Chavez. She came both to redeem her repentant children and to liberate them from the injustice and suffering imposed upon them.[56]

The three themes considered above reveal the Mexican-descent, Catholic kinetics as sublimely incarnational and relational. Their values, arising from the kinetics and expressed in these themes, include those of *respeto* and *vergüenza*, the experience of the world as divinely ordained but not rigidly ordered, and the belief that suffering is redemptive and liberating. Any treatment of conversion (intratraditional intensification) in this population therefore must include a description of how a member of this population might retrieve his or her world view (kinetics and values) as expressed in the formal, ritual behaviors discussed above.

A Description of Conversion

Most accounts of religious conversion use a stage-model description. I think that the spiral model developed by Orlando Costas is a more helpful construct for describing intratraditional intensification within this population.

Costas holds that conversion is a distinct, unique moment but also part of a continuous, dynamic, and complex process of returning to God. And for a Hispanic in the United States, three distinct and unique moments on the spiral must be: 1) conversion to Christ; 2) conversion to culture; and 3) conversion to world.[57] By "conversion" Costas means "a return to," "a recommitment," "a retrieval of." Conversion for a Hispanic in the United States must indeed mean a return to Christ (microcontext), but must also include a retrieval of his or her culture (mesocontext), and a recommitment to the world (macrocontext). These contextual conversions are often reactions to a felt crisis in that particular context, and rather than occurring in linear stages, they are dynamically interrelated. If, for instance, a husband loses his job and his wife is supporting the family, this is a complex crisis. In the macrocontext, the loss of one income might mean the stress of poverty. In the microcontext, the entire family can be upset because the traditional role of the male as provider is threatened, and the role of the female as domestic nurturer is made more difficult. And all of this could create a crisis in the mesocontext, opening the family to doubt their religious world view. The spiral model suggests the dynamic, interrelated character of crisis and conversion in this population. For the sake of description, however, I shall deal with each moment of conversion separately.

Conversion to Jesus Christ is certainly central to any Christian religious conversion. The challenge here for the Mexican-descent person is to be able to understand intellectually and reembrace affectively the kinetics of her or his popular spirituality. The realism of popular spirituality is based on a preenlightenment, sensual approach to Christ. The stress is on the corporate body of the Church somatically experiencing the events of the historical body of Christ.[58] Socialized into this nonverbal, nonrational, corporate, and affective relationship to an incarnate Christ, one is not encouraged to emphasize a personal relationship to Christ (outside of the corporate whole), just as one is not trained to think of a personal identity apart from, or outside of, the family and community. The kinetics of incarnation and relation are in metaphysical tension with the literal, individualistic, positivistic (re: modern) approach to Divinity found in the meso- and macrocontexts of the United States. Either this direct conceptual attack on the microcontext, or an indirect anomie caused by a crisis in the macro- or meso-contexts, can lead one to question the entire system of themes (rites and symbols), kinetics, and values that had been, until that moment, rather uncritically accepted. In other words, a crisis in the world view can challenge the efficacy of formal expressions (see figure 4), and conversely an attack on the formal expression can lead to serious doubts concerning the efficacy of the world view.

Intratraditional conversion to Christ in the microcontext means the individual must make a "quasi-sacramental act of personal confession . . . the outward means of express[ing] [a personal] commitment to Christ."[59] This may give us a clue to the success of such movements as the Cursillistas and the Charismatics.[60] Both groups are popular—sharing much the same anthropology, eschatology, and Christology as popular spirituality—but they adapt to the modern need for individual, public commitment to Christ. Intratraditional intensification on this level, then, would mean also making explicit and personal what has previously only been implicit and corporate: The Divinity lives among us (incarnation) and has given us many ways of encountering It (through relation), indeed wishes and desires our "centering." Conversion for this population on this level must include, then, an explicit intellectual and affective retrieval of the three values arising from its kinetics and expressed in the themes and rites of passage, incorporation, and revitalization in a way that allows and encourages one to personalize and publicly recommit oneself to this relationship within, but distinct from, the corporate whole. When the kinetics encoded in popular themes are personally appropriated and embraced, when the values these themes express inspire individual reorientation and rededication, when the themes themselves become a source of personal as well as communal spiritual reflection, one can say that the process of conversion to Christ within this population has begun.

The traditional, Mexican-descent population in the United States (microcontext) is ideologically Catholic. However, it often has an ambivalent relationship with the official personnel and structures of the Church (mesocontext) because the Church itself has a checkered history of ministering to it.[61] Despite a shared kinetics, the thematic structure of the Church in the United States is generally routinized, bureaucratic, and intolerant of the popular values of its own medieval past (from which springs popular spirituality).[62] Crisis on this level often includes a clash between the official structures of the Church and the expectations of the people. The Church in this country is highly influenced by modernity, and the resultant emphasis on individuality and comprehension of doctrine. Thus, the realistic, affective themes that fall outside its control are often barely tolerated; sometimes they are misunderstood or discouraged. There is a strong sense of order, planning, and punctuality—those who do not fit the plan are often left apart from institutional consideration. The complex hierarchy and mutuality of the Mexican-descent family is blithely judged unenlightened, its deeply Christian albeit popular spirituality (which mirrors family relations) is dismissed as superstition, and the poverty and discrimination it suffers (and which it com-

bats precisely through the symbolic subversion of popular spirituality) is simply ignored.[63]

Popular spirituality has endured for centuries despite official
Church absence or opposition. It seems absurd that a Church,
founded by immigrants and now consisting of various ethnic
groups, would still insist in actual practice if not in official docu-
ments on the assimilation of all members into what has begun to
look much like a civil religion. Certainly, the most urgent conversion necessary in the mesocontext is the conversion of Church
structures, an openness to being evangelized by the poor and
those of color.[64]

However, since the topic is conversion from within the Mexican-
descent, Catholic population, the necessary change in the mesocontext is a conversion to culture, an insistence on rediscovering,
celebrating, and reanimating the unique Catholic culture that is
theirs. A conversion to culture is a conscious and critical reappro-
priation of the values of a society, expressed in themes, in the
light of Christ. This is not to imply that only a few elite professionals can engage this conversion: Maria de la Cruz Aymes
proved this in her project "Fe y Cultura": The simplest person
can learn to think critically.[65] It is at this level, however, that the
ethos and the *pathos* of the community must be made clear, and
what is contrary to the Gospel must be challenged. A description
of conversion to culture must be twofold: at once a rediscovery
and celebration of the culture as the primary tool for evangelization, and a critical reappraisal of that culture in the light of the
God who evangelizes. If this were done throughout the mesocontext, including the level of official structures, we would see a
radical conversion indeed.[66]

Lastly, we have conversion to the world—the growing conviction that Christianity implies not only an ongoing personal, spiritual, and cultural conversion, but a mission to convert the
economic, social, and political order (macrocontext) as well.[67] This
moment in conversion has been reflected upon in liberation theology, and there is strong evidence to suggest that conversion on
this level deeply effects the intratraditional intensification of the
Mexican-descent population on the meso- and microcontexts as
well.[68] However, it is important to see this conversion in tandem
with the other conversions of the spiral. Divorced from culture
and the Christ of this culture, the mission to the world can be-

come abstract, narrow, rigid, simplistic, and corrupt. It is only by informing each conversion with the other that the process remains dynamic, integrated, and holistic.[69]

What would this conversion look like? If it includes a conversion to Christ from a popular approach, it would include a spirituality of martyrdom. Popular spirituality insists on accepting the will of God, even if this means suffering. However, this suffering is redemptive and liberating. Redemptive because through it we are conformed to the suffering of Christ, liberating because we ask the question: Is it God's will that God's children suffer injustice? The privileged role of the poor and humble in popular spirituality mirrors the subversive role this spirituality has played throughout history: While God wants to purify and commune with us through our suffering, God also wishes to raise up the lowly and bring justice to the world. Popular spirituality contains a strong sense of the Godhead as just and demanding—thus the mediating and placating roles of Mary and the saints. And its respect for suffering includes a respect for martyrdom, i.e. a willingness to suffer with God for God's people in the cause of justice.[70] Therefore, a conversion to the world will be a struggle to convert the world into that peaceable reign where the commandments of a just God will be respected, drawing upon the extant strengths in the culture as informed by Christ.[71] A conversion to Christ and to culture necessitates a conversion to the just God of Christ, and the cultural mandate to suffer with God in the struggle to midwife God's reign.

Another diagram is in order to complete the complex picture of conversion (figure 5).

The macrocontext is the whole figure, indicated by the long, bracketed horizontal line at the top. The mesocontext is the professional sector, the official Church structures. The microcontext is the centered set, with Divinity at its core. The dots with lines indicate individuals who are always influenced by each context at once (and by each other), and who are always in dynamic relation to the Divine, moving toward the center, or away from it. The large arrow emanating from the small spiral indicates one such person in the multifaceted, spiraling process of conversion toward the core of the culture, i.e. the Divine.

To indicate individual conversion within this complex process, I have placed a spiral emanating from one of these dots. The

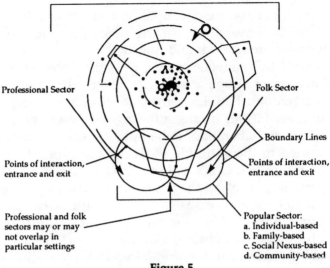

Professional Sector

Folk Sector

Boundary Lines

Points of interaction, entrance and exit

Points of interaction, entrance and exit

Professional and folk sectors may or may not overlap in particular settings

Popular Sector:
a. Individual-based
b. Family-based
c. Social Nexus-based
d. Community-based

Figure 5.

spiral has the three threads of conversion: to Christ, to culture, to the world. Each thread on the spiral creates a centrifugal force, moving the person away from the margin of the microcontext and more towards the centripetal force of the Divine. As the person moves closer to the Divine, the themes of popular culture become more meaningful, the values expressed more important, the kinetics more compelling. A strong, unifying world view develops that gives meaning and order to this person and to his or her community.

The initial energy for this movement is a crisis in one or more of the contexts. Perhaps the value of mutuality and hierarchy is challenged in the macrocontext when one is isolated from her or his family and community: A sense of isolation develops. Perhaps one has experienced discrimination from rigid and unyielding official Church structures: A sense of worthlessness and the desire to be assimilated may develop. Or perhaps one has been oppressed by the stress of unrelenting poverty and begins to doubt Our Lady of Guadalupe's promise to be a mother to the poor. Indeed, one may experience a complex crisis in each context simultaneously, or feel that a crisis in one context causes a reaction in another. In each case, the energy of change has been generated. If this change creates an unanswered spiral of stress, isolation, and assimilation, the person is eventually caught up in a vortex that pulls him or her farther and farther from the Divine. If, however, one can alleviate isolation by participating again in a rite of passage; if one can resist assimilation through a rite of revitalization; if one can find relief from daily stress in a rite of incorporation, then one has begun to find an antidote to the crisis in the world view of one's own culture, as expressed formally in these themes. This energy acts to "center" the person. When this energy is channeled towards the center rather than away from it, intratraditional intensification, or conversion, occurs. Three necessary, distinct but not separable, moments in this conversion are: conversion to Christ; conversion to culture; conversion to world. We know that conversion for this population must include an innovative adaptation of its themes so that its kinetics become more explicit, and its values personally and publicly reappropriated. We know that the culture must be evangelized (i.e. disabused of pathos), and it must itself evangelize. And we know that any conversion is incomplete if it does not respond to the call of a just God to make the Divine Reign of Justice a reality. This, then, is conversion in this culture: Responding to contextualized crisis by reinforcing existing values through a threefold recommitment to the essentially Christian world view of this people by means of an explicit, personal, and public retrieval of its kinetics, achieved by an innovative adaptation of its formal themes. The specific pastoral implications of this description of conversion is not yet a possibility: A more careful multidimensional, diachronic analysis must be attempted by the people and their leaders. Suffice it to summarize thus: If the aim of ministry is conversion, then ministry among this group will include whatever incorporates, confirms, and revitalizes the group's popular spirituality.[72]

Having explored the concept of conversion among the Mexican-descent, Catholic population, the next chapter endeavors to compare this description with the experience of conversion in Alcoholics Anonymous. I will be especially interested in the three core concepts: 1) respeto and vergüenza; 2) the experience of the world as divinely ordained but not rigidly ordered; and 3) the belief that the suffering, especially of the poor and humble, is redemptive and liberating.

3

Awakening the Spirituality of A.A.: Conversion in Context

Conversion is the key element in the treatment process of Alcoholics Anonymous. The Big Book calls it a spiritual awakening. But is this dynamic culturally peculiar, that is, can it speak outside of the white, anglophone, Protestant, middle-class milieu in which it was born? The purpose of this chapter is to build on the last and to see how conversion within A.A. is similar to the conversion process of the Mexican-descent Catholic (MDC). I use the same parameters as the previous chapter.

I have defined conversion (intratraditional intensification) within the MDC community as a response to a contextualized crisis that reinforces existing values (*respeto y vergüenza*, the world as divinely ordained but not rigidly ordered, and the redemptively liberating value of the suffering of the poor). It occurs through a threefold recommitment (Christ, culture, and world) to the essentially Christian world view of this population by means of an explicit, personal, and public retrieval of its kinetics (incarnational), achieved through an innovative adaptation of its formal themes (rites of passage, revitalization, and incorporation).

The macrocontext of the Catholic alcoholic is the larger world that labels him or her deviant. The microcontext is the A.A. fellowship. The mesocontext are those who mediate between the macro- and microcontexts: Those who either enable alcoholism (codependents), or those who enable recovery. The mesocontext includes family, friends, clergy, and pastoral agents.[2]

The microcontext of A.A., like popular spirituality, is a centered set. Although on the surface the defining center of A.A. would seem to be sobriety, in fact I shall show that the center of A.A.

is actually the Higher Power, as the Divine is the center of popular spirituality.

An analysis of conversion within A.A., as in the previous treatment of popular spirituality, must look at its kinetics (relation to the Divine), and its epistemology (what values are nurtured and how they relate to the kinetics). Although I am specifically interested in the religious aspects of conversion, I shall begin by drawing on insights from the medical, psychiatric, and sociological disciplines that have studied A.A., and then I shall turn to a comparision between the experience of religious conversion within A.A. and conversion as experienced within the MDC community.

Medical-Psychiatric Opinions

Since its inception, A.A. has been influenced by medical doctors. Carl Jung and Karl Menninger are perhaps the best known early advisors (although a cofounder of A.A.—Doctor Bob—was also a medical doctor). These luminaries were all involved in the evolution of A.A.. There are others, though, who have been more involved in its analysis.

The first of these was Dr. Silkworth, who identified two essential components of A.A.'s success: talk therapy (deviants "counseling" other deviants), and the experience of the A.A. fellowship as a new, nurturing community.[3] Using the five steps from the Oxford Movement (the precursor to A.A.), it was Dr. Silkworth who initially identified definite parallels between religious conversion and successful therapy with alcoholics.

Dr. Harold W. Lovell, in a paper presented to the American Academy of General Practice in 1953, built on Silkworth's analysis and called for a holistic treatment of alcoholism (physical, social, emotional, and religious). E. M. Jelline and others supported this controversial theory, but it was psychiatrist Harry M. Tiebout who presented the most convincing argument for this approach. Beginning with the 1943 meeting of the American Psychiatric Association, Tiebout began to expound on his theory of surrender. Surrender is what he called the "spiritual awakening" (conversion) that culminates in the twelfth step. Put simply, surrender means the conscious and unconscious desire to not dominate people or events. In A.A. parlance, surrender means accepting that the human is not God, and giving up reliance on one's own power. The Big Book identifies the ego of the defiant individualist as the root of alcoholism: Surrendering a life centered on self, in favor of one centered on others, is absolutely necessary to recovery. Tiebout's controversial claim in 1943 was that, logically, only a power greater than the alcoholic's narcissistic ego, i.e. a Higher Power, could supplant that ego. For this reason, I state that, at the center of A.A., as in popular spirituality, lies the Divine.

This view drew such controversy from psychiatric circles, and continues to draw it, that Tiebout spent the rest of his life defending and deepening this valuable insight.

First, he distinguishes between surrender and submission. Submission is conscious, intellectual acquiescence, but does not include unconscious, emotional acceptance. Surrender, on the other hand, is a holistic and complete end to resistance. It is the conceptual and emotional, conscious and unconscious conviction that the individual is not the center of the universe.

It is difficult to distinguish submission from surrender. An alcoholic may undertake actions that appear to be very selfless, and yet she or he may, at the same time, unconsciously hold on to great selfishness. Indeed, the process of conversion is often long and gradual, but the deciding factors are not just actions, but also feelings. Serenity is the hallmark of true surrender and acceptance—hence the importance of the serenity prayer to A.A.[4] Later, I shall show how A.A. has its own intrasystemic way of identifying mere submission and encouraging true surrender.

Tiebout used a Freudian framework to explain what he meant by true surrender (ego reduction). Specifically, he spoke of the reduction of the unmodified, infantile ego, not in terms of reducing its size but rather its object—self-love. Two essentials of this ego reduction are: 1) an unconscious renunciation of narcissism; and 2) a conscious trust of others. These essentials are predicated on the acceptance of the Higher Power, as Tiebout pointed out.[5]

According to Tiebout, religious conversion, or spiritual awakening, in A.A., is the act of surrendering one's reliance on one's own power. Because the power of the alcoholic ego is so great, the only thing that can supplant it is the acceptance of a Higher Power. Tiebout sketched the process of conversion in four steps. First, a crisis (anomie) jolts the defiant individual into facing the reality that she or he is not God. If no one enables the alcoholic to deny this reality, then the next step is surrender, if it is not death. This surrender leads to ego reduction and acceptance. Last, there follows a catharsis and overwhelming serenity necessarily manifested in selfless action. Although Tiebout saw conversion as a complex, often lengthy, and sometimes fitful process, these are the essential characteristics he identified.[6]

Doubt about the entire A.A. enterprise is still present among some of the medical and counseling professions, although the controversy is nothing like it was fifty years ago. Because of the work of courageous pioneers like Silkworth, Lovell, and Tiebout, we have a body of literature that analyzes conversion in A.A. from medical and psychological perspectives. In sum, it states that conversion is a change occasioned by a mental, psychical, social, or spiritual crisis, that results in a totally honest reassessment of the alcoholic's reality (conscious and unconscious, intellectual and emotional). This reassessment leads to the surrender of the power of the immature ego, and is necessarily predicated on the prior acceptance of a power greater than the ego, that is, a Higher Power.[7]

Sociological Opinions

Sociological studies of A.A. are a recent phenomenon. However, what little has been done to analyze conversion in A.A. from a sociological perspective is instructive.

Sociologically speaking, conversion is a change of identity rooted in the acceptance of another group's world view. One interprets one's past and present experience through the meaning-making system of a new group, and the plausibility of this new identity is reinforced by frequent contact with this same group.

The A.A. world view includes the acceptance of a Higher Power, and through this lens it interprets the experience of moral and spiritual regeneration. For instance, the identity of the individual alcoholic is changed from one of deviance to one of illness.

And the plausibility of this new identity, based on the A.A. system, is reinforced by frequent contact with A.A. fellowship, ceremonies, testimonies, and literature. From a sociological perspective, then, conversion within A.A. is a personal identity transformation resulting from an alcoholic in crisis (crumbling plausibility structures) accepting the world view, outlined in the twelve steps, and thus reinterpreting her or his reality from a new social context that legitimates him or her as a person.[8] I say conversion "within" (not to) A.A. because it is a systemic conversion. One remains an alcoholic—the conversion is within the continuum of recovery. As A.A. oldtimers are fond of saying, recovery begins the first time the alcoholic worries about his or her drinking. An alcoholic survivor, then, is always somewhere within the continuum of conversion, (even before initial contact with A.A.).

Sociologists contend, then, that A.A. is more than sobriety, it is a complete philosophy of life. Conversion is the personal redefinition of past and present experiences from the A.A. world view, and a lifestyle discontinuous with what A.A. considers past moral and spiritual degradation. As have the psychological disciplines, so sociology has also identified phases in this conversion.

First, the alcoholic experiences a crisis ("hitting bottom"): Past solutions fail and no one enables denial. Dim memories of previous positive relationships (family, Church, therapy) help the alcoholic avoid complete despair. This is the beginning of the continuum of recovery and conversion. Second, initial contact is made with A.A., a sponsor is adopted, and some bonding occurs. Third, the "pigeon" is given a sense of purpose by fulfilling some group responsibilities, and his cognitive acceptance of A.A. begins. Satellite organizations (Alanon, Alateen, etc.) insure the support of significant others. Fourth, the new identity is publicly accepted ("Hi, I'm Joe Smith and I'm an alcoholic"). At this point, mortification occurs and the moral inventory is shared, challenged, and finally affirmed, which signifies the individuals' subordination to the group. Fifth, testimony publicly affirms the new identity. Sixth, complete commitment leads to missionary zeal in spreading the A.A. news and strengthening the organization. Thus, a new, more respectable identity has been achieved, and a new community discovered in which to celebrate that identity.[9]

Having drawn on both the medical, psychological, and socio-

logical disciplines, I now turn specifically to the religious significance of conversion within A.A.

Comparing Conversion Experiences: A.A. and the Mexican-Descent Male

While the world view of A.A. includes practical moral guide-
lines, it is important to remember that at its center are ultimate
questions: life or death, addiction or liberation, and especially
self-centeredness or God-centeredness. Its concern with ultimate
issues, and its concomitant lack of rigid dogmas or institutions,
is key to A.A.'s universal appeal.[10] The wisdom of A.A.'s "spiritual
awakening" (conversion) is precisely its retrieval of the ancient
(re: traditional) sense of religious conversion as a public, not individualistic, event. That is why conversion in A.A. is a holistic
experience. It includes a cognitive conviction concerning certain
propositional truth claims (e.g., alcoholism is a disease), but it
also includes an experiential and unconscious animation evoked
by nondiscursive symbols. It is on this latter level that pluralism
prevails, and where culturally particular views of conversion are
completely possible.[11] Hence, conversion for the Mexican-descent,
Catholic alcoholic within A.A. can very well include, and I would
argue ought to include, an innovative, explicit, personal, public,
threefold recommitment to the kinetics expressed in the formal
rites (that is, their peculiar symbol system). Herein lies the challenge of the pastoral agent as cultural broker: reframing the symbol system of the MDC to animate especially emotive,
unconscious conversion within A.A.[12]

This is entirely appropriate because A.A. and Mexican-descent
Catholic popular spirituality share remarkably similar kinetics
and epistemology.

Recall that I have identified the MDC kinetics as incarnational:
they reject rigid demarcations between secular and sacred.
Rather, Divinity is experienced as dwelling intimately with us,
sharing our time and space, and as the source of our life as well
as the goal of our destiny.

A.A. shares this incarnational (though not necessarily Christian) kinetics. There is a deliberate melding of the secular (therapeutic) and sacred (religious) spheres in their experience of

conversion. This tension is necessary, primarily because A.A. deals with ultimate issues (religious sphere), and insists that the alcoholic ego decreases while surrender to the Higher Power increases. Yet, at the same time, A.A. espouses certain opinions (e.g., alcoholism is a disease) more in keeping with therapeutic than religious disciplines. In addition to this melding of sacred and secular (incarnational kinetics), A.A. tolerates a great ambiguity of religious expressions. Any variety of organized, corporate (or unorganized, individual) articulation and celebration of this experience is acceptable. It is precisely this rejection of rigid boundaries between sacred and secular, religion and science, that explains why neither radical positivists nor religious fundamentalists embrace A.A.: It refuses to fit neatly into any accepted category.[13] However, it is certainly true to say that, for A.A., the Higher Power is the source of life (sobriety) and the goal of destiny (selflessness). Moreover, there is a shared sense of the immediacy of this nebulous Power: The second tradition claims that It is the only and ultimate A.A. authority. It refers to the Higher Power as a loving presence whose will is known through the consciousness (indwelling) of the group. Thus, while not literally believing that the Divine took on human flesh, as orthodox Christians do, A.A. shares kinetics that can be heuristicly described as incarnational.

The epistemology of the MDC nurtures certain values, among them: 1) *respeto* and *vergüenza;* 2) the belief that the world is divinely ordained but not rigidly ordered; and 3) a conviction that the suffering of the poor and humble is redemptive and liberating. Again, one can point to parallels in A.A. epistemology.

Mutuality is at the core of the nonprofessional therapeutic approach of A.A. Everyone in the fellowship is at once helped and helping, no one is a healed healer. Rather, all are recovering and helping to rehabilitate others. Likewise, there is a hierarchy, not between individual A.A. members, but between the objects of each ego. As Tiebout points out, a converted A.A. member has surrendered her or his ego to the Higher Power. Now recall that it is both *mutualismo* (between members) and hierarchy (between members and the Divine) that are at the heart of the MDC values of *respeto* and *vergüenza.* A.A. emphatically preaches respect for self and respect for others, and believes that an alcoholic ought to be allowed to suffer the natural consequences of his or her actions (guilt and shame) when she or he violates that respect. Therefore, like the MDC, A.A. both proscribes and prescribes behaviors that nurture the values of *respeto* and *vergüenza* (through the twelve steps and twelve traditions).

The concept of serenity is the A.A. way of expressing a world that is divinely ordained but not rigidly ordered. A serene person believes in a Power that ordains reality, and therefore has the confidence to leave to that Power that which the individual cannot control (e.g., alcoholism). Yet fatalism is nowhere in evidence. A.A. teaches "it's not your fault, but it is your problem." In other words, while there is no freedom with regard to addiction, there is freedom in choosing recovery. Like the MDC, A.A. believes that our natural, healthy destiny is the Divine. Both world views accept the freedom of the individual to either cooperate with this destiny, or to egotistically (and uselessly) strive against it. Both also believe in the value of a healthy, harmonious relationship to a world that is essentially good and that invites not our defiance but our participation. It is because the world is divinely ordained that the alcoholic can accept the Divine and can trust in creation. Yet, because it does not believe that the universe is rigidly ordered, A.A. embraces all expressions of religious experience.

Hitting bottom is the first and essential moment in the recovery of the alcoholic. So long as she or he is able to deny reality and maintain his or her plausibility structures, she or he will never seek help. Each person must experience the humiliation and degradation of deviancy (different for each individual), in order to risk not just submission but true surrender. As A.A. old-timers say: "I believe my promises, but I obey my pain." It is this suffering that is liberating (from alcohol) and, at least for the Catholic alcoholic, redemptive. The worst thing that a codependent can do is shield an alcoholic from the natural, logical consequences of her or his actions. "The gift of pain" is the first step towards sobriety and salvation. Hence, it is true to say that A.A. also sees the redemptive value of suffering, especially among the marginated (deviants), and believes as well in pain as a necessary step toward true liberation, (surrender).

As I said previously, for the MDC "suffering is an essential part of centering," that is, centering on the Divine. This is equally true of the alcoholic: Suffering is essential to surrendering, placing the Higher Power, rather than self-love, at the center of the ego. This is such a strongly held belief that it is the accepted way of identifying mere submission and encouraging true surrender. "Tough love," "getting at the truth," and "working the program" are all code terms for confronting, and thereby causing varying degrees of suffering for, one who hasn't really made a complete moral inventory, one whose testimony smacks of nostalgia for the past, or one who is being otherwise less than scrupulously honest and humble. The fellowship of A.A. is based on sharing "experience, strength, and hope," but if that experience is hedged, or the hope phony, one is confronted. This brutal honesty is nothing less than a conviction that, just as only the suffering of logical consequences of past actions got one into A.A., so only the continuing suffering of total honesty will keep one liberated from alcohol, and open to God's redemption.

In effect, religious conversions as experienced in MDC popular spirituality and in A.A. share marked similarities. Both depend on the public, explicit, and personal retrieval of the values outlined above. Therefore, they share a common epistemology and kinetics. Both experience conversion as a complex process that includes the emotional as well as cognitive faculties, as one moves toward the Divine, the center of the universe both of Alcoholics Anonymous and of Mexican Descent Catholics. MDC intratraditional intensification is a return to, or retrieval of, the values contained symbolically in its rites. A.A. likewise provides a symbolic structure through which one can retrieve the identity of that acceptable, nondeviant person who lived before being warped by addiction. Both retrievals are occasioned by a crisis. In each case, the mesocontext (for the MDC, the Church; for A.A., codependents) can play either a very positive role in mediating between the micro- and macrocontexts, or can effectively enable the macrocontext to destroy the microcontext. For both populations, conversion is communal and voluntary, and at the center of both is the universally intuitive experience of the Divine, or Higher Power. For this reason, I believe it accurate to say that the religious conversion that is essential to the treatment modality of Alcoholics Anonymous is completely harmonious with the concept of religious conversion among the Mexican-descent, Catholic population in the United States.

4

A Project for Pastoral Agents

At this point in my research, I felt confident that indeed Alcoholics Anonymous could be, and ought to be, adapted to the reality of the male, Mexican-descent Catholic. I had identified some of the challenges and specific ways in which to encourage the inculturation of A.A. In other words, I knew the who, what, and how—what I lacked was the when and where to test these findings.

Objective

The objective of my project was to test the hypothesis that pastoral agents could indeed learn about and use A.A. as a resource in their ministry. I had produced a manual, or lesson plan, based on the previous research of chapters 1 through 3, that met this objective.

Background

My first step was to identify existing ecclesial agencies through which such a project could be launched. It seemed useless to reinvent the wheel (i.e., locate classrooms and office space, and begin advertising) if such had already been done. I chose a representative, urban, Catholic diocese in California that has, as part of the department of catechetical ministries, an organization, or "Instituto," that promotes the training and continuing education of Hispanic pastoral agents. Currently, it has five parish-based sites in which some twenty different classes are offered.

I contacted the coordinator of the Instituto and we met about my offering a class, based on the manual I had written, as part of the curriculum of the Instituto.[1] The coordinator was very interested and accommodating. She also made several helpful suggestions. For instance, I had planned on taping only the final half-hour of each class, a time set aside for discussion. She suggested that people would talk more freely if I taped the entire class, so that by the time the last half-hour expired most people would have forgotten about the tape recorder.

With her valuable assistance, therefore, in the Fall of 1990 the Instituto offered a class on alcoholism, which I taught on Tuesdays (4 September–13 November from 7:00–9:30 P.M.) at a suburban, multicultural parish. The class was based on the manual I had prepared, and was to be a test of its effectiveness.

Although the site and other preparations were provided by the Instituto, I took it upon myself to do some additional promotion. I know through personal experience that general announcements in church get a general response—a communal yawn. However, personal invitations from the pastor, or others who coordinate local ministry, elicit a much better response. Therefore, on 1 August 1990 I wrote a letter to all the pastors and coordinators of the twenty-one parishes in that diocese who celebrate Mass in Spanish (appendix A). Afterwards, I made a phone call to each person, and on 22 August I sent out another letter (appendix B). The Instituto's coordinator also sent a brochure to each pastor, who also received all the regular mailings from the diocese concerning upcoming events and opportunities.

This was a time of flux in the diocese. A number of the pastors were on vacation, and several others were in transition from one assignment to another. However, through persistent effort I was able to contact nineteen of the twenty-one. The first letter was meant to catch their attention; the second was rather more informative. Both were sent in hand-addressed envelopes to give them a personal touch.

I am convinced that this strategy of "personalismo" is why we had a reasonable response to the class. Almost all the students had been invited by the local coordinator of Hispanic ministry; only one had responded to a general announcement. The cost of the course was not prohibitive ($20), and about half of the students either could not pay or were subsidized by their respective parishes.

Class Profile

The makeup of the student body was interesting and informative. Although the class dealt specifically with males, men comprised only thirty percent of the class. Ninety percent were in their forties, and all of them were foreign born (virtually all Mexicans). Considering this, a rough measure of their level of acculturation revealed what would be expected: They are bilingual but prefer Spanish, and although they are better educated and more prosperous than their parents, they tend to maintain close ties with their country of origin and its traditions. This information was ascertained by means of a questionnaire (appendix C). The questionnaire itself was based on consultations with the Instituto coordinator, members of my doctoral board, and previous work I had done under the direction of Dr. Carlos Muñoz of the University of California at Berkeley.[2]

The questionnaire was administered to see if the student body was generally representative of the Mexican-descent Catholic population as a whole. And indeed it was. It also afforded a very helpful profile of the students (see figure 6).

Class Agenda

The class was structured (e.g., we always closed with a prayer led by a student), yet fluid. Students brought their spouses and children, often a friend, and tardiness and absenteeism were constant challenges. I was able to identify ten of the most regular students, and used them as the basis for the study. However, all of these ten missed at least one class.

On the first day, after explaining what I hoped to accomplish, I asked them to help me with the evaluation of the class. I assured them that their confidentiality would be respected, but that since the class was part of my doctoral project, I needed to systematically measure the effectiveness of the course. They agreed to allow

	1	2	3	4	5	6	7	8	9	10	Participants
1	X	X	X								Male
1				X	X	X	X	X	X	X	Female
3	X										-30
3		X	X	X	X	X	X	X	X	X	+30
4	X	X			X	X	X	X	X	X	+Education
4			X	X							-Education
5			X		X	X	X	X	X	X	Barrio L
5	X	X		X							Barrio M
6	X	X	X	X		X	X	X	X	X	Married L
6					X						Married O +
7		X	X	X	X	X	X	X	X	X	Friends L
7	X										Friends O
8	X	X	X			X		X	X	X	Visit 5+
8				X	X						Visit 5-
9		X	X	X	X	X	X	X	X	X	Food L
9	X										Food M
12	X	X			X	X	X	X	X	X	+$
12			X	X							-$
13		X	X	X	X	X	X	X	X	X	Spanish Yes
13	X										Spanish No
15		X		X		X		X			Mexicano/a
15					X		X		X		Hispano/a
15	X		X							X	Mex-Amer

(left axis label: QUESTION NUMBERS)

Figure 6. Only those questions from appendix C that were *not* unanimously answered are here included. To question three, all answered foreign-born. To question ten, all answered Catholic; to eleven, all said they want their children to be bilingual; and to fourteen, all pray in Spanish. Terms with which *no one* identified in question fifteen are omitted in the chart. An "X" marks each response, "1" signifies "latino"; "m" signifies "mixed"; "o" signifies "other"; a plus sign means "more," and a minus sign means "less." The chart, correlated to appendix D, offers a detailed portrait of each of the ten participants. Thus, participant one is a male, under thirty, better educated than his parents, married to a Latina, but whose friends are mostly non-Latino. He visits his country of birth infrequently, eats a variety of food, makes more money than his parents, prefers to speak English socially, and identifies himself as a Mexican-American.

the class to be taped and evaluated by members of my doctoral board and to fill out a questionnaire (appendix D) that evaluated their knowledge of alcoholism and Alcoholics Anonymous. It covered one side of a legal-size piece of paper, and it took some twenty minutes for them to complete it.

The group averaged twenty-six percent correct answers. Many of them had never heard of Alcoholics Anonymous (although one was a member), and most of them shared the common myths concerning alcoholism. I discuss the significance of this finding in the following chapter.

It was also during this first class that I explained that a further requirement would be attendance at some twelve-step group concerned with alcoholism. They could attend A.A., Alanon, Alateen, or A.C.O.A., but they had to attend at least two meetings, and reflect on the experience with the class. A brief introduction of the theme of alcoholism concluded this first session.

In the second class, I spoke concerning alcoholism as it is manifested in the adult, male, Mexican-descent population of the United States. I touched upon the importance of the role of the pastoral agent in reaching out to these persons, particularly those who are Catholic, and addressed those issues that the previous questionnaire clearly indicated were necessary (e.g., alcoholism is a disease, not a character fault).

It was in the third class that I spoke at length about Alcoholics Anonymous, and the promise that I felt it held for the Mexican-American community. These first three classes were based on chapter one, "A.A.: Making it User Friendly."

Afterwards, I listed the twelve steps of A.A. and spent about an hour discussing the significance of each, always attempting to cast it in a way helpful to the pastoral agent, and illuminating for those of Mexican-descent. For instance, for the third step, the moral inventory, I adapted the dissertation of Rosendo Urrabazo and summarized twelve positive aspects of machismo.[3] I deliberately kept the language simple, and stopped often for questions.[4] I did not use the terms "conversion" or "popular religiosity," but the concepts were incorporated. Popular religiosity was broached in the discussion of the Higher Power. Conversion was constantly addressed by such A.A. sayings as "Being a drunk isn't your responsibility; recovery is."

Two classes were devoted to processing the experience of vis-

iting a twelve-step group. This was very valuable for both procedural and personal reasons. Procedurally, it helped the students
learn how to make a referral. They had to locate the appropriate
meeting, investigate its specifics (e.g., if it were in Spanish, for
men only, etc.), coordinate transportation, and actually learn the
rudiments of how a twelve-step meeting is run. Personally, it
was enlightening, since many of the students discovered that the
skeleton of alcoholism indeed occupied the dark recesses of one
of their familial closets. They learned and processed a live experience that no class or book can provide, and this gave them a much
richer and deeper understanding of alcoholism and its treatment.
Now, in their role as pastoral agents, if someone asks them "what
happens at one of those meetings?," they can answer from experience. They began to have both the tools and the conviction necessary to make meaningful referrals.

The complete text of each class was distributed one week in
advance, and before beginning a new theme, I always briefly reviewed the concepts introduced the previous week. The students
were encouraged to read the A.A. *Big Book*, and many related
pamphlets were also distributed.

At the end of each class, at least one half-hour was devoted
to free discussion. Beverages and snacks were served, and the
atmosphere was one of mutual trust (if not always relaxed). Sometimes the discussions were directed (e.g., after the required visits
to twelve-step groups we discussed that experience), but generally the students themselves proposed and answered the questions.

The last class was devoted to a discussion concerning how the
students could use what they had learned. The idea was to elicit
their own understanding of themselves as pastoral agents. Although they never used the words "cultural broker" or "catalyst,"
they expressed the concepts in their own way. Two women said
they wanted to begin a Spanish-speaking Alateen (there is none
in that area). One woman had already spoken with her pastor
about being a resource to him when he encountered alcoholism
in the parish. Two men said they would either distribute A.A.
literature or have someone come and speak about alcoholism at
Mass. They all exchanged ideas and learned from each other.

Despite the students' eagerness to use their newly acquired
knowledge and experience, there was some anxiety about dealing

directly with alcoholics. Therefore, we did some role-playing, and each took a turn "trying on" his or her new skills.

Lastly, I administered to them the very same questionnaire they had answered on the first day (appendix D). This time they scored seventy-eight percent correct answers; previously, they had correctly answered only twenty-six percent. At their insistence, we also agreed to meet sometime the following semester and compare experiences, or even begin a support group. As the last class broke up, people were exchanging addresses as well as ideas: a bond had developed between us after so many hours of confident, open discussion.

One may notice a discrepancy between the number of classes initially proposed (13), and the number actually held (11). The last two classes were canceled, after consulting with both the Instituto coordinator and the students, for two reasons. First, we had entered the holiday season, and since the students were all involved in their parishes, plans for Thanksgiving and Advent were beginning to demand more of their time. Second, I had completed all the material I had intended to teach, and felt it was time that they return to their pastors and prepare to integrate themselves into a holistic parish ministry.

In the end, each student had a copy of the manual, an experience of a twelve-step group, some ideas on how to incorporate this into their ministry, and a core group of persons who were committed to the same endeavor. The following chapter will evaluate the efficacy of this accomplishment, and point to some areas that require further investigation.

5

What Flew, What Failed

The evaluation (EVALUAR) of the project outlined in the prévious chapter takes several parts. First, a reflection on the background preparation for the class. Second, a brief quantitative analysis based on the questionnaires. Third, a qualitative reflection from each of the two doctoral board members who listened to tapes of the classes. And finally, my own reflections and suggestions for future research.

Reflection on the Background

I believe it was a wise move to work through existing ecclesial structures, although this presented its own difficulties. Despite these challenges, presented below, the enormity of doing all the advertisement and preparation without this support, and without many personal contacts, would have been too daunting in such a brief period of time and with no other support or funding. If a different, well-known, and well-financed institution could have been utilized (e.g., Minorities Alcoholic Treatment Alternatives), it is possible that the preparatory stage would have been more fruitful and less frustrating. However, since the population I wished to test was Catholic, it seems fitting that I experience both the pains and the joys of working with those Catholic institutions that my students (pastoral agents of this particular diocese) experience every day.

The Instituto coordinator was always wise, helpful, and encouraging, an essential part of the entire process. She helped me fine-tune the testing instruments and plan the lessons. I could not have asked for more competent and eager support.

However, the Instituto she heads, as part of the diocese at large, was under severe strain just as I began my project. As in many Catholic dioceses across the country, hers also was in the middle of "strategic planning," a strategy that often results in downsizing diocesan offices and parishes.[1] Hence, at the time I turned to the diocese, its outreach to Hispanics had been reduced from four full-time positions to one and one-half positions. Other budgetary constraints rendered the usual advertisement done by the Instituto less effective. And generally, the morale of the persons engaged in Hispanic ministry was at a low ebb. Therefore, all preparations for the class were less effective and more difficult than they would have been in previous years.

Moreover, it was an exasperating experience to convince the priests of the diocese to cooperate. Those religious sisters, and lay persons charged with Hispanic parochial ministry, all without exception, responded favorably. Getting the priests to encourage and support students for the class was much more difficult. Being a priest, I understand their reluctance to take on yet another project. That is precisely why, in my letters to them, I tried to emphasize how this endeavor was meant to aid their ministry and save them time in the future by preparing co-workers to help them. Their response was tepid.

It is easy to interpret this lack of enthusiasm as justification for the usual priest-bashing, and indeed I am tempted. There are, however, mitigating circumstances. First, as in most Catholic dioceses, the priests who minister to Hispanics are by and large overworked, unappreciated by their superiors, misunderstood and isolated from their colleagues, and frustrated by certain actions of the Chancery. They also suffer from the debilitating effects of "strategic planning." Moreover, I contacted them in August, a traditional month for priests to take vacations; many others were in the midst of being transferred to other assignments and therefore were not at liberty to begin new projects. Finally, I must admit that I have little personal rapport with those diocesan clergy. I am not a member of the caucus of priests engaged in Hispanic ministry, and know only about a third of those engaged in that ministry. Thinking back, I believe that had I known the clergy personally, and had I approached them at their meeting rather than through a rather impersonal letter (like the hundreds they receive weekly), their response probably would have been more supportive. This is an important point because their support (financially and morally) is usually the linch-pin in any new effort at Hispanic ministry in the Catholic Church.

Because the class was a nonaccredited, volunteer, lay-centered effort, its structure was not that of a university course. The students all worked and had families, and this, rather than disinterest or irresponsibility, was the reason for their tardiness and absenteeism. It is possible that more encouragement on my part—a phone call asking why a student had been absent—would have lessened these problems. But I was dealing with adults, and I am not sure that that would have been either appropriate or helpful.

The classes were structured but "messy." As noted above, spouses, children, and friends came and went, snacks and drinks were served, and the conversation was rather free-flowing and often intense. Again, I realize that this affected the content of the class: Students' attention to lectures may have strayed due to these comings and goings, and important points may have been missed. I am convinced, however, that given that particular student body, this "messiness" was most conducive to learning. Generally, Hispanics are more adept at dealing with several persons at once, and do not make such clear demarcations between work and leisure as do I.[2] Dealing with each individual, taking the time to speak politely to them, and making allowances for differences, is very important. A genuine sense of welcome and warmth is as important as a well-prepared lecture. Since my goal was to create a learning environment for these individuals, rather than to set up a classroom atmosphere most conducive to myself, what I consider a "messy" structure was, I hope, a natural and comfortable experience for my students.

One could certainly question the seeming contradiction of a young, gringo priest teaching a group of older, Hispanic laity how to be good lay ministers. This, however, was never my intent. I accepted their self-definition as pastoral agents, and consequently their dignity and maturity. Many a time I digressed from a prepared lecture to ask their advice about a question of ministry. However, our topic was specifically ministry to the alcoholic, and in that respect I did have more preparation than my students, and something valuable to teach. I do believe that we all learned and that the process was as egalitarian as possible. Indeed, it may have been precisely because the students were engaged in ministry that they were more likely to take direction from a priest without either dismissing him with anticlerical prejudice or fawning over him with uninformed submissiveness.[3]

Analysis of Questionnaires

Two questionnaires were used to do a simple, quantitative analysis of this project. The shorter of the two attempted to determine if this class was relatively representative of the Mexican-descent Catholic in the United States.

The predominance of women within the churchgoing community is certainly representative. The number of alcoholics and co-dependents was also representative (one in six). The group may have been a bit old for a Mexican-American community, but not so much if we consider only churchgoing Catholics. Indeed, the only major concern resulting from this survey was the fact that *all* the respondents were foreign-born.

First, it is important to remember that the class was taught and the manual written in Spanish. Since it was monolingual Spanish, one could have presumed that more foreign-born (as they are usually more proficient in Spanish, and less in English) would attend. Second, thirty percent of the respondents were first generation secondary immigrants, that is, adults who had come to this country as the dependent, minor children of first-generation, primary immigrants. Of those, all identified themselves as Mexican-Americans. Discounting the one non-Mexican in the group, fully one-third of the students consider themselves Mexican-Americans. This is relatively representative of the Spanish speaking, Catholic, Mexican-descent community in the United States. Parenthetically, if we consider only the male respondents (and the study is for the male alcoholic), two-thirds of the males identify themselves as Mexican-Americans. At the very least, the class was representative of the churchgoing, Catholic, Spanish-speaking, Mexican-descent community of the United States.

The other questionnaire was longer, testing the class' understanding of alcoholism and Alcoholics Anonymous before the first lecture and after the last one. Before taking the class, the students scored only twenty-six percent correct answers ("fatal," as one of the students described it). After eleven weeks they scored seven-

Students

1	2	3	4	5	6	7	8	9	10	
X	X	X								#7 correct
			X	X	X	X	X	X	X	#7 incorrect
										#3 correct
X	X	X	X	X	X	X	X	X		#3 incorrect

Figure 7.

ty-eight percent correct answers, a threefold increase. Obviously, the class had a significant, positive effect on the students' understanding of the issues.

However, seventy-eight percent correct answers is still little more than a passing grade; almost a quarter of what they currently know and may share in their role as pastoral agents is suspect. The students themselves seem to have been acutely aware of this, and they asked for some continuing support. Indeed, they have since called me for advice. Additional readings outside of class may have helped improve this score, but I tend to think that the graver mistake was skipping the last two classes. Although I had reviewed all the material I had prepared, we could have used these classes to *process* what we had studied, and specifically to emphasize those aspects that the questionnaire had disclosed that the class had not understood. Given the time constraints mentioned in the previous chapter, perhaps another time of the year (where such important celebrations as Our Lady of Guadalupe would not impede pastoral agents from taking the full course), ought to be explored.

The two questions still most often misunderstood by the class at the end of the course (see appendix D) were number seven of the true-and-false, and number three of the multiple-choice. Figure 7 identifies each participants' responses to these questions.

Number seven states that one cannot become an alcoholic if all one drinks is beer. This is a common misconception, reinforced by advertisement,[4] and particularly prevalent among Latinos, where containment of drinking, rather than control of it, is the common way co-dependents react. In other words, no one denies the male his right to drink—controlling or refusing him drink is a more typically white, nonHispanic response. Rather, the family and friends of the Mexican-descent alcoholic intervene to *contain* his drinking. They may attempt to convince him to drink only wine or beer, or to drink only on weekends, or only in the cantina and not at home. It is not surprising, then, that this question is still misunderstood, and probably reflects that I needed to confront this peculiarly *Latino* denial technique more forcefully.

The third multiple-choice question dealt with the ultimate authority in A.A. (which is a Higher Power). I believe this failure was due to the class not reading the Big Book, as had been suggested. Attendance at twelve-step meetings and reading the Big Book were all explained as essential to understanding A.A. Then again, this book *is BIG*—a fact that may have discouraged the students from reading it. Much of the essential of A.A. (see chapter one on the essential and potential of A.A.) is summarized in its many simple, readable pamphlets, virtually all of which are translated into Spanish. It may have been wiser to have assigned these two- and three-page pamphlets as weekly homework assignments. This quantitative evaluation is necessary and helpful, but so also is a qualitative measure. Therefore, I now turn to that portion of this chapter.

Evaluation of Indigenous Professionals

Doctor Melville is a Chicana anthropologist at the University of California at Berkeley. Father Allan Figueroa Deck is a missiologist at the Jesuit School of Theology at Berkeley. They are both nationally recognized leaders and experts on the Mexican-descent population in the United States. They both agreed to listen to tapes of the classes and to offer their opinions. I met separately with each of them on 6 December 1990, and their evaluation appears below.

Both evaluations were generally very positive. The class discussions showed that the students had been able to apply what they had learned to their own life situations, had been able to internalize the principles involved, and could express them in their own words. The discussion questions were well-phrased and appropriate to the particular class, and it seems I gave helpful clarifications and additions when needed.

Both professors appreciate that the topic of alcoholism is a very delicate one, and not conducive to a solely lecture-based format. The rather free-flowing exchange that occurred, therefore, was probably both healthy and unavoidable. I was particularly pleased that they felt I had done a good job of addressing with sensitivity the peculiar needs and gifts of the Mexican-descent community.

A few people, especially women, seemed to dominate some of the discussions, which raises the question as to whether a different dynamic should have been used. Fr. Deck asked if perhaps a better pedagogical model would have been to segregate the group by sex, at least some of the time. This is a time-honored Catholic and Hispanic way of encouraging unity and, therefore, frankness in a group. Perhaps if this had been done at some point, the men would have been more participative.

There also seemed to be a certain amount of "Father Knows Best" hesitation at times. People would discuss their opinions, followed by a pregnant pause, waiting for the priest-instructor to approve. However, I was able to defuse this practice and return the students to the discussion of their own views.

Lastly, while it was noted that the verbal evaluation of the class by the students was helpful and instructive, it may have been more helpful to ask them to write their evaluation of the class.

Dr. Melville saw the manual (lesson plan) as a helpful handout that would be an excellent future reference. The lectures elaborated on this presentation and offered practical suggestions for its application. The lectures were well prepared, relevant, and yielded good discussion among the students. The students themselves were representative of the larger population, and responded well to the themes and images juxtaposed between MDC culture and A.A. They seemed to understand the importance of religion in this juxtaposition. Dr. Melville thought that my own status as a priest (as well as my experience with MDC culture and language) made me an appropriate presenter of just such a juxtaposition. Hence the adaptation of A.A. to the MDC culture was done in a careful and thorough manner.

If the class were to be presented again, Dr. Melville suggests that the manual be reviewed, the process of selection and sponsorship of students from within the diocese be re-examined, and that a follow-up phase be offered in which class participants would be supervised in implementing in their own locale what they learned. She touches upon these observations in her preface to this book.

Father Deck agreed in the main with these observations. The manual and class presentations were well received, as evidenced by the easy *confianza* that developed. Because the Hispanic senses of time and learning are distinct from those of mainstream North Americans, the "messiness" of the schedule was quite appropriate.

The themes and images used were especially appropriate, and showed a remarkably successful effort to integrate the cognitive, factual aspects of alcoholism with the affective, religious, and spiritual aspects of the problem as experienced within the Hispanic cultures. Fr. Deck complimented me on my efforts to effect an "insiders" view of the culture.

Fr. Deck went on to remark that while the oral evaluation was good, a more formal, written evaluation of the class would have provided me with something more tangible for reflection and therefore possible adjustments. Specifically, more must be done to recruit and animate men for the class; perhaps talking to them one-on-one would encourage them to be more forthcoming. Finally, Fr. Deck agreed with Dr. Melville that some kind of follow-up to the class would be helpful and would indicate the true impact of the class (beyond the experience of the pastoral agents) on the Church at large. I have included their valuable critiques in the published version of this manual.

Personal Reflections and Suggestions

My own opinion of the class is also quite positive. I was impressed by the willingness of these modest, hard-working people to travel a considerable distance after work to attend a class that prepared them, not for paid positions, but only for more volunteer labor in the Church. I was touched by their confidence in me as their instructor and their willingness to cooperate with this project. I noted their capacity to discuss very personal matters, and the implied trust in their fellow ministers.

The students' own positive, verbal responses, and their eagerness to apply what they had learned in achievable, concrete ways in their local communities, was very complimentary of the class.

At the same time, they were not starry-eyed idealists,—rather, they were mature veterans. Therefore, they were not afraid to mention their fears and doubts, and indeed asked for some kind of continuation. I believe that the fact that the students continue to telephone me for advice and support, and I them, speaks highly of the class.

Contemporary Hispanic ministry in the Catholic Church today is both a rewarding and draining experience. Such was this class. Extant ecclesial structures, while necessary, and to some extent helpful, were also painfully slow in reacting. Yet many of the individuals in these institutions were exceptionally talented and generous.

The class itself was sufficiently representative of the population as a whole, and measured enough increase in understanding the dynamics of alcoholism and its treatment, that I consider it a success. In the future, the full semester of classes ought to be utilized, and A.A. pamphlets be required reading. At least one class should be segregated according to gender, and then the students themselves should be allowed to decide whether such segregation was helpful. Some personal contact with Catholic clergy would result in greater moral and financial support, a *sine qua non* in this ministry; after all, the students will have to return and learn to work with their pastors. Lastly, frequent, written evaluations of the course, and a measure of student understanding, would allow the class to emphasize those aspects it most needs to address. Attention to content precisely tooled to the class, and a plan of instruction appropriate to it, need always be considered.

Recall that I am a frog in my field, neither Hispanic nor a blissfully ignorant anglophone, but an amphibian trying to negotiate both worlds. As a friend writes, ". . . in whichever direction we go, one side of us limps."[5] This project was both exhilarating and frustrating. Exhilarating because I learned so much and enjoyed significant success. Frustrating because I am continually reminded that I am an outsider. As much as I understand intellectually the importance of Our Lady of Guadalupe for instance, she is still not an unconscious, meaning-making myth for me. That is why I made the mistake of originally scheduling classes that conflicted with this celebration and its preparation. Although I have studied assiduously the Mexican-descent male, the intercultural dynamics of gender relationships is still a subtle undercurrent I fail to grasp. And I still experience some anxiety concerning the "correction" of certain MDC myths, such as those surrounding drinking (e.g., only beer). Reframing these myths is something that must be done with great care, and with the participation of the members of the culture themselves.

It is not self-pity I am identifying, but reality. I live in and minister to a Church often divided and searching for its own identity. I am therefore pulled in these various directions and am forced to continually reexamine my identity as a minister to this particular Church. It is a frustrating business. At the same time it is exciting and innovative. Each time I seek to reframe the myths of this culture (in this case those concerning alcoholism) I am reframing myself. Besides my own personal continuing quest, the following areas, at the intersection of alcoholism and the MDC culture, are in need of further research.

In the first chapter I identified acculturation as a predictor of alcoholism. However, measuring acculturation and understanding its complex effect is still a field in need of considerable investigation. As I state in chapter two, a multidimensional, diachronic analysis of conversion from within this population is also long overdue. Such efforts might answer the nagging questions: Why is A.A. more widely accepted among Latinos outside of the United States than among those in this country? How ought we to evaluate more precisely the ethos and pathos of this community? What about adapting other twelve-step groups (e.g., Narcotics Anonymous, Parents Anonymous, Gamblers Anonymous)?[6] These are all questions eminently worthy of further consideration and future study.[7]

6

Conclusion: Of Frogs and Princes

I began work on this project some four years ago. The statistics and reflections that have emerged since then have only served to confirm my reasons for exploring the connections between the Mexican-American and Alcoholics Anonymous.

The key to this effort is the ability to juxtapose in the imagination of the people the meaning and making of symbols of both A.A. and the Mexican-American. This is what will reinforce the necessary conversion, or change. And the unique role of the pastoral agent is precisely to use his or her acceptance in each community in order to do this juxtaposition.

First, we need recall the meaning-making system of the Mexican-American Catholic. The symbols I have identified in chapter two (with the values therein encoded) continue to capture the popular imagination. Witness that when the Academy of Catholic Hispanic Theologians of the United States wanted to thematize Hispanic popular religiosity they chose to consider the cultural symbols of Mary and the Cross.[1] The values that are expressed in these symbols are many and complex, but among the most important of them are those of *respeto and vergüenza*, the world as divinely ordained but not rigidly ordered, and the belief that suffering is both redemptive and liberating.

Second, in chapter three, I demonstrate that the values of these symbols are values also of A.A. My research made clear to me that the key conversion experience can be inculturated precisely because of the affinity of these shared values. A.A. preaches self-respect and respect for others and proscribes and prescribes behaviors that nurture this respect. Likewise, the concept of serenity is the A.A. way of recognizing that the universe is divinely ordained (therefore, the confidence of leaving to God what we cannot control), yet not rigidly ordered—there is no fatalism, but

84

rather confidence in one's ability to recover. Finally, A.A. has always seen suffering as the beginning of recovery (liberation).
"Hitting bottom" is the time-honored way of identifying when
one had finally begun to respond to the "gift of pain" and climbed
back towards a life of freedom.

Third, chapter one had made clear the essential role of the
pastoral agent. The pastoral agent (especially a recovering alcoholic or one in Alanon or Alateen) is the mediator between these
two similar but as yet still mutually unfamiliar groups (A.A. and
MDC). As a cultural broker and as a catalyst, the pastoral agent
has the unique dual role of relating both to the spirituality of
A.A. (the center of this "centered set") and to the cultural reality
of the Mexican-American, which also revolves around the Divine.
As an accepted member of each group, his or her role is unique
and crucial. This is the reason for the separately published handbook mentioned in the preface. I did not want my work to remain
solely on the level of the English-speaking, scholarly world.
Rather, I wanted to place it within the reach of those who could
turn this theory into reality, i.e. the pastoral agents in the Church.
It is they who instinctively understand the sublimely relational
and incarnational kinetics of the people, and who, with some
formation, can understand and communicate the similar epistemology between their people and A.A. Hence, as I show in the
two closing chapters, they are the ones who can act as native
resources to the microcontext, which always exists in tension
(creative or destructive) with the macrocontext. They are also the
hope for the mesocontext, as they do healthfully what the mesocontext sometimes does dysfunctionally, that is mediate between
the micro- and macrocontexts.

The keys to this investigation, and to the future of the Church,
therefore, are the pastoral agents. They are the new Church—
those bilingual and bicultural ministers who work in concert with
the whole Church to create a world Church at once both universal
and particular.[2] As a pastoral agent myself, I have found in these
past twelve years that indeed it is possible to navigate between
different cultures. It is possible when people of good will respect-
fully critique their own culture in light of the Faith, and enter
into dialogue with each other. This investigation concerning the
inculturation of A.A. (begun in a white, anglophone, Protestant,
middle-class community) with the Mexican-descent, Catholic

community, is a modest attempt, at a manageable level, of demonstrating that point. Mexican-Americans continue to be the largest single group of U.S. Hispanics; close to 63% of all Latinos are of Mexican descent. Mexican-Americans remain poor; almost twenty-five percent exist below the official poverty level.[3] These recent statistics demonstrate yet again the need for an inculturated treatment modality that can serve especially the largest group of Catholic Hispanics and yet remain within their economic reach. A.A. can do this. I like to think that this project is just the beginning. A.A. is the grandparent of dozens of very effective twelve-step groups in the anglophone world. If it can be inculturated among the Mexican-Americans, what about other groups? Domestic violence (often related to alcohol) is widespread.[4] So is drug abuse, incest, and other compulsive behavior problems addressed by other twelve-step groups. My dream is that this project may be the start of many more.

It is my privilege and my joy to be doing such ministry, even as a cultural amphibian, a bridger of dissimilar worlds. I realize that we "frogs" often create warts and slime through our well-intentioned mistakes. That is why careful analysis and critique is essential. Nevertheless, it is a worthy adventure when it is done in the faith that, with the kiss of the Prince of Peace, all such frogs will eventually turn into princes.

Appendix A

Dear Father: 1 August 1990

<u>THIS IS NOT ANOTHER REQUEST FOR YOU TO SOLVE A CRISIS;</u>
<u>THIS IS AN OFFER TO HELP YOU SAVE TIME IN YOUR MINISTRY.</u>

I too am a parish priest in the diocese working mainly with Hispanics.
When I noticed that much of the counseling and crisis intervention which I did was rooted in alcoholism (e.g., domestic violence,
child abuse, economic difficulties), I decided to make the treatment of
alcoholism among Hispanics the project of my Doctor of Ministry
program.

I hope to help priests like you and me by offering a course to train
lay, Spanish-speaking members of your parish to be able to diagnose
and intervene in alcoholic families. Think of what a help it would be to
us if we had trained, trusted persons in the parish to whom we could
refer those who come to us with alcohol-related problems. I will offer
this course through the Tepeyac Institute this September, and you can
contact the director or me for more information.

This letter is just to encourage you to invest a few moments this
month with two or three of your parishioners to personally invite them
to take the course. It is not for persons who are alcoholics (unless they
are recovering), but for persons who are committed, compassionate co-
workers you would trust to work with you in the future. I guarantee
that a few moments of your time invested in this personal approach
now will save you much time in the future as these persons begin to
take on much of the problems caused by alcoholism that now wind up
in your office.

I'll be honest with you: I need your help. Without sufficient students,
I can't teach the course. But I'm also honest when I say I chose to teach
the course (after my own extensive training and research) because I see
the need, and I want to help the average parish priest like you and I
respond to this need without demanding more time from us. We all
believe in lay collaboration; this is another way for laity to help us minister better without burning ourselves out.

I'll be calling you later to remind you of this letter, once the Tepeyac
Institute mails out its Fall brochures. Won't you keep this letter on hand

and begin to consider who you might encourage to take this practical, helpful course? Thank you for your time and attention.

Sincerely in Christ,
Fr. Kenneth G. Davis

P.S. If you're interested, I've outlined what I hope to do in the latest issue of *Apuntes: Teologia Desde el Margen Hispano.*

Appendix B

Dear Father, 22 August 1990

Peace and greetings in the Lord! You may recall our phone conversation today, as well as the letter I sent to you on the first of the month.

As I have explained, I will be teaching a course at the Tepeyac Institute called "Una Respuesta Católica al Alcoholismo Hispano" for lay or deacon ministers in your parish who are interested in learning how to help the Spanish-speaking alcoholics of your area.

The course will be taught every Tuesday night from 7:00 to 9:30 p.m.; a pulpit announcement *with a map of the location on the back* is enclosed for your convenience. You may copy it to give to people you think may be interested, and please do use it for your bulletin and pulpit announcements.

The first class is offered on September 4, and the last class will be held on November 27. A nominal fee is charged, as is explained in the folder which the Tepeyac Institute will be mailing to you.

I would greatly appreciate your encouraging two or three of your parishioners to at least come out and investigate the course; I believe it will be helpful to them, and in the long run for you, as they will be able to do some of the work you now do with alcoholic families.

Thanking you in advance for your kind cooperation, I remain

Sincerely yours in Christ,
Kenneth Davis, O.F.M., Conv.

enclosures

Appendix C

POR FAVOR DIGAME UN POCO SOBRE USTED. PONGA UNA "X"
EN EL ESPACIO *DESPUES* DE LA RESPUESTA MAS ADECUADA.

1) Usted es hombre _____, o mujer _____.

2) Su edad es menos de treinta _____, entre los treinta y los
cincuenta _____, mayor que los
cincuenta _____ años.

3) Usted nació en E.E.U.U. _____, o fuera de los
E.E.U.U. _____.

4) Usted tiene más educación escolar que sus
padres _____, o tiene igual o menos educación
escolar que ellos _____.

5) Usted vive en un barrio latino _____, o usted vive en
un barrio no latino _____.

6) Usted es, o había sido, casado con latino/a _____, o es casado
mejor con un no latino/a _____.

7) La mayoría de sus amigos son latinos _____, o no
son latinos _____.

8) Usted visita su país natal a menudo (es decir por lo menos
una vez cada cinco años) _____, o usted visita con
menos frecuencia _____.

9) Usted come generalmente comida latina _____, o usted
come una gran variedad de otras comidas _____.

10) Se supone que usted es católico. Esto es
correcto _____, o es incorrecto _____.

11) Prefiere usted que sus hijos sean bilingües _____,
o prefiere más bien que solo hablen inglés _____.

12) Económicamente, usted está en mejores condiciones que como
estuvieron sus padres _____, o usted está en peores condiciones _____.

13) En la vida social, usted prefiere hablar el
español _____, o el inglés _____.

14) Cuando reza o va a un sacramento, usted prefiere el
    español _____, o el inglés _____.

15) A usted le gusta más que le diga mexicano/a_____
    latino/a_____, hispano/a_____, chicano/a_____,
    méxico-americano/a_____, americano/a_____.

NO ES NECESARIO PONER SU NOMBRE. TODA LA INFORMACION
ESCRITA SERA ESTRICTAMENTE CONFIDENCIAL. MIL GRACIAS.

Appendix D

PARA MEJORAR EL CURSO, ME GUSTARIA SABER QUE PIENSA USTED SOBRE EL ALCOHOLISMO. POR FAVOR CONTESTE LAS PREGUNTAS SIGUIENTES. NO ES NECESARIO PONER SU NOMBRE. MUCHAS GRACIAS.

Usted es HOMBRE_____MUJER_____
Su edad es MENOS DE 30_____; ENTRE 30 Y 40_____; MAYOR DE 40_____

Circule la "SI" para decir que es cierto o la "NO" para decir que no es cierto

1. Si un homber ama a su familia, no se emborracharía. . . SI. . . NO

2. Los alcohólicos generalmente viven en la calle, pidiendo limosna para poder seguir tomando. . . . . SI . . . NO

3. Para dejar de tomar, lo mejor es prometer a sus seres queridos ya no tomar, y cumplirlo . . . . SI . . . NO

4. Nadie puede negar a un hombre su derecho de tomar . . . SI . . . NO

5. El alcoholismo es una enfermedad . . . SI . . . NO

6. Los alcohólicos siguen tomando porque no tienen la voluntad y el valor necesario para controlar su manera de tomar . . . SI . . . NO

7. Uno que solo toma cerveza o vino jamás será un alcohólico . . . SI . . . NO

8. Un alcohólico puede controlarse y volver a tomar de vez en cuando sin problema . . . SI . . . NO

9. A.A. quiere decir "Asociación de Automóviles" . . . SI . . . NO

10. Los doce pasos se refieren al Santo Via Crucis . . . SI . . . NO

Circule la letra que corresponde a la respuesta Mejor.

1. El grupo "Alcohólicos Anónimos" propone creer en: a) La Iglesia Católica; b) La Cristiandad; c) un Poder Superior; d) que no existe Dios; e) no se

2. El único requisito para poder pertenecer a los Alcohólicos Anónimos es: a) que sea uno borracho; b) que sea uno sobrio; c) que lea su literatura; d) que tenga el deseo de no tomar; e) no se.

3. La autoridad fundamental de los Alcohólicos Anónimos está basada en: a) su líder debidamente elegido; b) un Dios amoroso; c) el comité central; d) sus escritos; e) no se.

4. La meta principal de los Alcohólicos Anónimos es: a) lograr que nadie tome; b) educar al público que el alcoholismo es una enfermedad; c) llevar su mensaje al alcohólico que sigue sufriendo; d) prohibir alcohol a los menores de edad; e) no se.

5. Alcohólicos Anónimos se mantiene por medio de: a) sus propios recursos no más; b) donaciones del gobierno; c) dinero de la Iglesia; d) venta de licor; e) no se.

Notes

Introduction: On Being a Frog in My Field

1. By "marginated" I describe those who are socially, culturally, politically, or economically on the margin of society, i.e., structurally disenfranchised from centers of power.
2. Davis, "We're Not in Kansas Anymore."
3. "CORHIM: Hispanic Seminars." This same journal publishes my annual report "U.S. Hispanic Catholics: Trends and Recent Works."
4. Widely accepted as the father of contemporary U.S. Hispanic Catholic theology, Elizondo's work revolves around the concept of the double *mestizaje* or mixture experienced by the Mexican-Americans. First there was the forcible mixing of Spanish and Native American races (1492–1821), then the forcible mixing of these people with Anglophones (1836 to the present). The result, according to Elizondo, is a double sense of rejection. The Mexican-American is rejected by Mexicans as "pochos," "cholos," etc., and by Anglos as "beaners." See Elizondo's many entries in the bibliography.
5. Rogers, *Cold Anger.*
6. One needs to be acutely aware of the ancient wisdom that "Translators are traitors." Hence the use of the neologism "inculturation," which is used here to mean the dynamic relation between a message (e.g., A.A.) and a culture (e.g., Mexican-Americans) resulting in an integration of that message into that culture through an ongoing process of respectful, reciprocal and critical interaction between them. See Azevedo, *Inculturation and the Challenges of Modernity.*

Chapter 1. A.A.: Making It User Friendly

1. Gilbert, "Hispanic Americans," 58. Henceforth this population will be referred to as Mexican-Americans. See also Burnam, "Prevalence of Alcohol Abuse."
2. Caetano and Medina-Mora, *Immigration, Acculturation and Alcohol Use,* 28. Caetano's later works appear to strengthen the thesis that acculturation is positively associated with alcoholism. See also Orlandi, *Cultural Competence for Evaluators,* 94. For dissenting opinions, see the December 1990 Supplement to the *American Journal of Public Health.* Acculturation is that process of adapting from one culture to another, measured by such factors as bilingual capability, fertility rates, intermarriage, income, and education.
3. Alcoholism is here defined as a chronic disease, or disorder of behavior, characterized by the repeated drinking of alcoholic beverages to an extent that exceeds customary dietary use or ordinary compliance with the social drinking customs of the community, and which interferes with the drinkers' health, interpersonal relations, or economic functioning. Late stages of alcoholism, or "low

bottom" drinkers, are characterized by lengthy intoxication, tremors and early morning sickness, a neglect of food, physical deterioration, and finally a complete physical and mental breakdown. Taken from Masi, "Occupational Alcoholism."

4. See Caetano and Medina-Mora, *Immigration,* 59. Also Malone, *Report of the Secretary's Task Force,* 159. And D. R. Panitz et al, "The role of machismo and the Hispanic family in the etiology and treatment of alcoholism in Hispanic American males."

5. Gilbert, "Mexican-Americans in California."

6. Dobkin De Rios and Feldman, "Southern Californian Mexican-American Drinking Patterns."

7. Particularly lacking are studies of the Mexican-American woman and elderly, as well as studies of alcoholism among other Hispanics. What little is known suggests that acculturation is associated with heavier drinking because of the anxiety felt when one experiences the incongruity of both capitulating to the dominant class's cultural myths, and confronting the impossibility of achieving this goal. A related hypothesis holds that the reversal of the majority of Mexican-American males to more acceptable drinking patterns may be due to the voluntary and involuntary inhibition exhibited when drinking with "liberated" (i.e. acculturated) wives and other significant females. See Gilbert, "Lifestyle Integration of Alcohol Consumption."

8. Spanish-Speaking Mental Health and Research Center, *Emotional Support Systems. Curanderos* (folk healers) are not frequent resources for the cure of alcoholism.

9. Casté and Blodgett, "Cultural Barriers."

10. A good example of this questioning attitude is exhibited in Munoz, "Chicano Alcohol Counselor," 86–87. The debate continues in Gilbert, *Alcohol Consumption Among Mexicans and Mexican-Americans.*

11. An exegetical eye will note that the only emphasis added to any of the Twelve Steps deals with the Higher Power. Italicized are the words *as we understood Him.* These steps, the twelve traditions, and the Big Book make up the constitution of A.A. One will note that the majority of this contains suggestions, not dogma. To receive A.A. literature, write to Alcoholics Anonymous World Services, Inc., P.O. Box 459, Grand Central Station, New York, NY 10163.

12. See traditions eight and nine. Deliberations by this board are almost always suggestions, and may be altered easily as the membership of the board, and the needs of A.A., change.

13. Lusero, *Alcoholics Anonymous in a Chicano Community,* 127.

14. *Time* reported the first groups in the former Union of Soviet Socialist Republics (10 April 1989). See also Robinson, "The Growth of Alcoholics Anonymous."

15. The A.A. General Service Board lists 251,000 members in Latin America. Of these, 202,000 are Mexican. In North America 720 Spanish-speaking groups are listed. The first one, dating from 1945, is still operating in Los Angeles.

16. Many of these translations, while technically correct, are cumbersome and are, therefore, often locally adapted. Also of note is the fact that A.A. usually began very slowly in the Latino milieu, often only coming into its own with the creation of its own Service Board, and often with the aid of local professionals and celebrities. For a discussion of A.A. growth in Mexico, see Kenaston, "Sketch of the History of Alcoholics Anonymous in Zacatecas, Mexico," and Miguel Ramirez Bautista, *Comunidad Sin Fronteras.* For a U.S. hispanic perspective, see Gordon, "The Cultural Context of Drinking and Indigenous Therapy."

17. Alcocer, "Quantitative Survey," Table 65. Also Rootman and Moser, *Community Response to Alcohol Related Problems*, 96.

18. Trice and Roman, "Sociopsychological Predicators of Affiliation with Alcoholics Anonymous", 161.

19. Gilbert and Gonsalves, *The Social Context*, makes note of the importance of group bonding in this drinking, and the necessity to provide a similar group affiliation for the new abstainer. A.A. provides this fraternity.

20. The family develops its own problem-termed codependence, a symptom of which is the containment strategy mentioned above. The Mexican-American codependent female may respond differently than her anglo counterpart. She is often less cognizant of the existence of a problem, more long-suffering, less likely to intervene or to seek help outside her kinship circle. She will be less likely to try to control the quantity of drink consumed as to try to spatially contain her husband's drinking. She may manipulate domestic affairs such that he does not drink at home or appear intoxicated before her children. She may well seek the counsel of a pastoral agent. See Gilbert, "Mexican-Americans in California," 272–74.

21. This "deflation at the depth" is the source of any spiritual conversion, certainly not an impossibility for Mexican-Americans. And this recognition of interdependence (i.e., acceptance of the fact that one's actions have familial and societal repercussions) is also at the root of the cultural mutuality mentioned above. Lastly, this healing of relationships becomes the source for true self respect when one begins the reciprocity of helping others: "Ex-deviants may be uniquely qualified to aid in reintegrating deviants because they are usually accepted by both deviant and conforming elements of society" (Leavitt, *Social Issues and Communication*, 22, 167). Paul Antze deals with this conversion from the "omnipotent self" to the "accountable self" in a perceptive article that, while not dealing directly with Mexican-Americans, is really a classic description of the deviant macho who returns to the true and positive essence of machismo (Antze, "The Role of Ideologies," 330–31).

22. For an example of how this is being done, see Arredondo, Weddige, Justice, and Fitz, "Alcoholism in Mexican-Americans." The universal effectiveness of A.A. may be because alcoholism is a *disease*, and, therefore, "The folk forms of A.A. are shown to address presumably culture-free aspects of the biology of alcoholism" (quoted from Rodin, "Getting on the Program").

23. Ernest Kurtz, *A.A.: The Story*, 209. Although A.A. has shared the general human penchant for prejudice, it has become more and more open to the varieties of human experience. Its long ambivalence toward special interest groups (e.g., polysubstance abusers) has never stopped local fellowships from specializing in specific populations. This grass roots attitude was sanctioned in 1987 with the decision that such groups are indeed A.A. so long as their reason for existence is to maintain their sobriety, and provided they do not exclude other alcoholics. See page 208.

24. Two related studies of interest: Spanish Speaking Mental Health Research Center, *Delivery of Services*, shows the surprising degree of acceptance enjoyed by Chicano nonprofessional therapists among Mexican-Americans. An essay by Arnold A. Herrara and Victor Sanchez in the Spanish Speaking Mental Health Research Center's *Psychotherapy with the Spanish-Speaking*, notes the success of therapy groups that are "relatively didactic, goal-oriented, behavioral." This description is consistent with A.A., which avoids introspection and psychotherapy.

25. Although A.A. is itself nonprofessional, it has always drawn on the exper-

tise of professionals—from William James to Carl Jung. Latinos are no exception. The growth of A.A. in Latin America (and consequently among Latino immigrants to the U.S.) has had the public support of clergy, doctors, and others in public service. I use the term "local notable" in the sense coined by Cornelius in *Interviewing Undocumented Immigrants.*

26. Geller, "Alcoholics Anonymous and the Scientific Model."

27. "Pastoral Agent" refers to those bilingual and bicultural lay or ordained members of the Church who perform their ministry in a manner coordinated with, and integral to, the mission of the whole Church. See National Conference of Catholic Bishops, *The National Pastoral Plan for Hispanic Ministry.*

28. Research shows that, while there was initially some questioning (e.g. the dialogue between Fr. Paul O'Connor, S.J. and Dr. F. J. Braceland recorded in the *American Ecclesiastical Review* 106, nos. 3–4 [1942]), Church leadership swiftly embraced A.A., c.f. *Alcoholism: A Source Book for the Priest* (Indianapolis: NCCA, 1960).

29. Alibardi, *Recovery Process in Alcoholics Anonymous*, 13, lists the essentials of A.A. as: (1) a desire to stop drinking; (2) a personal analysis and consequent adjustment of personal relationships; (3) dependence upon a Higher Power; and (4) willingness to work with other alcoholics. Those listed are a compilation of current opinion.

30. Weber and Cohen, *Beliefs and Self-Help*, 352–53.

31. A.A. publishes newsletters specific to clergy and other professionals.

32. Bassin, "Proverbs, Slogans and Folk Sayings."

33. A good summary of the role of the folk therapist or "natural helper" (i.e., a model for the A.A. sponsor) is provided by Vallen and Vega, *Hispanic Natural Support Systems*, 39–94, 109. A.A. is specifically mentioned as an example of natural, indigenous healing.

34. Matthew 13:52 quoted from *La Biblia Latinoamericana* (Spain: Verbo Divino, 1972). In this discernment it may be well to pray: "God, grant me the serenity to accept the things I [ought not] change, courage to change the things I can, *and wisdom to know the difference.*"

Chapter 2. A Return to the Roots: Conversion and the Culture of the Mexican-Descent Catholic

1. Walter, "Conversion," 233–35.

2. Kenney et al., "Identifying the Socio-contextual Forms."

3. A few studies have dealt with conversion from one denomination to another, however, only one author, Juan Lorenzo Hinojosa, has dealt with intratraditional conversion (re: recommitment) from a Catholic, Hispanic perspective. Unfortunately, this work is not yet sufficiently developed to provide a complete model. See his chapter in Deck's *Frontiers of Hispanic Theology in the United States.*

4. Deck, *The Second Wave*, calls this a "moving target." The particular rites I consider in this study are those "religious folk practices" reported by González and La Velle in *The Hispanic Catholic in the United States.*

5. Lewis R. Rambo discusses several aspects of conversion, including that of tradition: ". . . . the social and cultural matrix that includes symbols, myths, rituals, worldviews, and institutions." By intratraditional intensification, then, I mean a recommitment to the social and cultural matrix through a retrieval of

the symbols, myths and world views contained in the rituals of this same concrete social and cultural context ("Conversion," 73).

6. For a discussion of a heuristic, holistic model see Rambo, "Conversion: Toward a Holistic Model of Religious Change."

7. Espín, "Grace and Humanness."

8. Rambo, "Conversion: Toward a Holistic Model," 52.

9. Elizondo, *Galilean Journey.* This *mestizaje,* of course, began in the United States in 1513, making it the oldest Christian faith expression in the country. Elizondo has created a seminal theology concerning this term, and seems to try to answer the criticism that his analysis is not radical enough (re: André G. Guerrero and Ada María Isasi-Diaz) in his newer book *The Future is Mestizo.*

10. Taken from Pérez, *Popular Catholicism.* I am aware that the terms "popular religiosity," "popular Catholicism," etc. are not coterminous with popular spirituality; I prefer the latter, as it seems less pejorative. Due to the constraints of space, the fact that scholarly opinion is divided over these issues, and because my aim is precisely to spark further debate and investigation, I do make certain (I believe defensible) generalizations in my presentation.

11. Roberto Goizueta has eloquently shown the inherent illogic involved in any dichotomy between popular (re: community) and institutional church. See "Nosotros: Toward a U.S. Hispanic Anthropology."

12. Garcia and Espín, "'Lilies of the Field,'" 74.

13. Ramírez, *Fiesta, Worship and Family,* 25.

14. Both the concept and the diagram of the centered and bounded sets (Figure Two) are taken wholesale from Hiebert, "Conversion, Culture and Cognitive Categories."

15. By *ethos* I mean the goals of a culture that drive or motivate prescribed behavior; by *pathos* I mean those attitudes and behaviors that, although often widely accepted and defended, are really at odds with these cultural goals. For an excellent analysis of the pathos and ethos of the Mexican-American community (i.e., machismo) see Urrabazo, *Machismo: Mexican-American Male Self Concept.* See also Buezas, "Mitos, Rituales y Simbolos."

16. Figure four and the concepts introduced in the following paragraphs are my adaptations of illustrations and ideas taken from Jacobs, "Culture and the Phenomena of Conversion."

17. Skansie, *Death Is for All,* 52–55.

18. Ibid., 56–57.

19. Ibid., 58–59.

20. Ibid., 122f.

21. Glazier, "La Muerte."

22. Ruiz, *The Days of the Dead.*

23. Ibid., 18.

24. Ibid., 32.

25. I am aware that this distinction between shame and guilt has been challenged, but I still believe it useful in this context. See Gerhart, *Shame and Guilt.*

26. The concepts of *respeto* and *vergüenza* are very complicated. This resume is taken from Kutsche, "Household and Family in Hispanic Northern New Mexico," and from Valdez, "Vergüenza."

27. Moore, "The Death Culture of Mexico and Mexican-Americans," 75.

28. Ibid., 82f.

29. Ada María Isasi-Díaz, "'Apuntes' for a Hispanic Women's Theology of Liberation."

30. Zazueta, *La Muerte y los Muertos,* 43. For a more complete account of what

I try to explain here, consult Orlando O. Espin's wonderful article "The God of the Vanquished: Foundations for a Latino Spirituality."

31. See Guerrero, *A Chicano Theology*, 158f. Recall that since 1848 the Mexican-descent population of this country has lived under the territorial and ideological domination of their anglophone conquerors. By passive aggression I mean the resistance and resentment expressed in both social relationships and occupational activities in response to this excessive, imposed dependency. I do not refer to a personality disorder that occurs only when direct expressions of hostility are available but not availed; with minority groups, direct attacks upon dominant structures are often not available, as they would be suicidal.

32. Parker, "Popular Religion and Protest," 29.

33. Elizondo, "Popular Religion as Support of Identity."

34. Skansie, *Death Is for All*, 145.

35. See for instance Patrick McDonnell's article "I 'Believe in Juan Soldado: Soldier Executed in 1938 Revered,'" in *The Los Angeles Times*, 5 November 1988, 6–7.

36. Romano V., "Charismatic Medicine, Folk-Healing, and Folk-Sainthood."

37. In the urban context, relational time becomes even more important. Great public feast days are not possible when a barrio, unlike a village, does not share a common relationship to a patron saint. Urban rites of revitalization become more private and personal (relational), i.e. celebrations of important anniversaries or the *quinceañera* (an obvious exception to this rule being the feast of Our Lady of Guadalupe—a testimony to her particular importance). The time of these celebrations is movable because they are not linked to a cyclical calendar but to important social relationships. See Galilea, *Pastoral Popular y Urbana*.

38. Ocampo, "Biblio-Hemerografía de las Fiestas y Ferias Populares."

39. Turner, "Mexican-American Home Altars."

40. Regis Jesuit Community, *Santos and Saints*, especially 91, 139.

41. Barbancho, "Santuarios y Peregrinaciones," 555.

42. See Adams, "Political and Economic Correlates of Pilgrimage Behavior," and also Neira, "¿Tiene la Religión una Función Alienadora?"

43. This quote is taken from Cinquino-Argana, *Economic and Religious Organizations*, 324. See also 310–23.

44. Isasi-Díaz, "'Apuntes' for a Hispanic Women's Theology of Liberation," 66.

45. The essence of Mexicanism is devotion to Guadalupe.

46. "A new moment that does not eliminate the preceding, but rather brings it to fullness." Translated from Triacca, "Tiempo y Liturgia," 1974.

47. Elizondo, "La Virgen de Guadalupe."

48. Taylor, "The Virgin of Guadalupe in New Spain."

49. Kurtz, "The Virgin of Guadalupe and the Politics of Becoming Human." "Liminal" from the Latin *limus* or boundary refers to a beyond-the-normal-boundaries experience of space and time.

50. See Campbell, "The Virgin of Guadalupe and the Female Self-Image," and Bushnell, "La Virgen de Guadalupe as Surrogate Mother in San Juan Atzingo."

51. Elizondo, *La Morenita*.

52. Campbell, "The Virgin of Guadalupe," 14–17. See also Stevens, "Marianismo: The Other Face of Machismo."

53. Wolf, "The Virgin of Guadalupe: A Mexican National Symbol."

54. Siller A., "Anotaciones y Comentarios al Nican Mopohua."

55. Siller A., "Para Una Teologia del Nican Mopohua."

56. Elizondo, "Mary and the Poor."

57. Costas, "Conversion as a Complex Experience."

58. I understand that this is a generalization. Remember that such is necessary in this brief treatise, and that I attempt only a synchronic description. However, I believe my position here to be tenable. See Galilea, *Religiosidad Popular y Pastoral Hispano-Americana*.

59. Costas, "Conversion as a Complex Experience," 26.

60. See Marcoux, *Cursillo, Anatomy of a Movement*, especially the treatment of "the fourth day," or ongoing conversion. Also Newman, "Charismatic Movement Gains Among Catholics." *The New York Times*, 1 March 1992: L28.

61. Sandoval, *On the Move*. See also Miller, *Mexican Folk Narratives from the Los Angeles Area*, especially 14–20.

62. Williams, *Popular Religion in America*, 17. Although this book does a poor job of treating specifically Mexican-descent popular religion, it is a good general introduction to the topic of popular spirituality.

63. There is a wealth of documentation on this issue. Two examples: Marin and Gamba, *Expectations and Experiences of Hispanic Catholics and Converts to Protestant Churches;* also Elizondo, "The Hispanic Catholic Church in the USA." However, it is not my intention to portray a dichotomy but rather a dialectic in the order of Goizueta's "Nosotros: Towards a U.S. Hispanic Anthropology."

64. Matovina, "Liturgy, Popular Rites and Popular Spirituality."

65. See Aymes et al., *Effective Inculturation and Identity*, 3–27.

66. This is one of the points emphasized by Abalos in *Latinos in the United States*. See especially his chapter on "Latinos and the Sacred."

67. Costas, "Conversion as a Complex Experience," 30.

68. Ortiz, "Chicano Urban Politics and the Politics of Reform in the Seventies." Cadena, "Chicano Clergy and the Emergence of Liberation Theology."

69. Mannion, "Cultural Fragmentation and Christian Worship." This is partly why I believe Rambo's framework to complement the spiral model of Costas.

70. This popular spirituality of martyrdom is eloquently expressed in the life of Cesar Chavez. See the essay about him in Mitchell, *Critical Voices in American Economic Thought*. For a discussion of popular spirituality as a resource for liberation theology, see Candelaria, *Popular Religion and Liberation*.

71. Galilea, "La Raiz de Nuestro Presente."

72. El Niño de Tlaxcala is a devotion to a statue of the baby Jesus, which is supposed to wander playfully through the town but that always returns to Church. This could serve as a metaphor for ministry: a festive ability to engage the world, while always returning to its roots. See Turner and Turner, *Image and Pilgrimage in Christian Culture*, 71–73. For an inquiry into contemporary Catholic ministry among this population, see *U.S. Catholic Historian* 9, nos. 1–2 (Winter/Spring 1990).

Chapter 3. Awakening the Spirituality of A.A.: Conversion in Context

1. Davis, "Return to the Roots."

2. National Conference of Catholic Bishops, *National Pastoral Plan for Hispanic Ministry.*

3. A.A. Worldservice, *A.A. and the Medical Profession.*

4. Tiebout, "Surrender Versus Compliance in Therapy."

5. Tiebout, "Alcoholics Anonymous—An Experiment of Nature."

6. Tiebout, "The Act of Surrender."

7. Wilson, "Sobriety."

8. Petrunik, "Seeing the Light."

9. Greil and Rudy, "Conversion to the World View of Alcoholics Anonymous."

10. Wyatt, "What Must I Believe to Recover?"

11. Bullock, "Public Language, Public Conversion."

12. Davis, "A.A.: Making It User Friendly."

13. Rudy and Greil, "Is Alcoholics Anonymous a Religious Organization?"

Chapter 4. A Project for Pastoral Agents

1. This manual is published separately as *Cuando El Tomar Ya No Es Gozar.*

2. The texts I used to prepare this questionnaire were: Gamio, *Mexican Immigration to the United States;* Keefe and Padilla, *Chicano Ethnicity;* and Martinez and Mendoza, *Chicano Psychology.*

3. Urrabazo, *Machismo.*

4. My vocabulary was intentionally limited to that of a primary school graduate. Any word I could not find in the *Breve Diccionario Porrúa de la Lengua Española,* I either omitted or defined.

Chapter 5. What Flew, What Failed

1. See Davis, "Base Communities," and Deck, "The Hispanic Presence."

2. Condon, *Good Neighbors.*

3. Lampe, "Is the Church Meeting the Needs of Hispanics?" Although I disagree with Lampe's conclusions, I agree with two of his insights that are germane to my point. First, practicing Hispanic Catholics have a generally positive opinion of priests, and educated (re: pastoral agents) Hispanic laity are more likely to critique priests. My students were neither anticlerical expatriates nor noncritical lambs.

4. See Perry Lang's article "Targeting Minorities Assailed," in the *San Francisco Chronicle,* 10 December 1990, A1 and A12.

5. Méndez, *The Way is Made in the Walking,* dedication page.

6. See my article "Child Abuse in the Hispanic Community: A Christian Perspective."

7. Some of these questions were answered at the Marin Institute, when the International Collaborative Study of Alcoholics Anonymous presented the results of its four-year analysis of A.A.

Chapter 6. Conclusion: Of Frogs and Princes

1. See their newsletter, volume 2, number 1 (Winter 1990).

2. This idea is borrowed from Elizondo, *The Future is Mestizo.* A friend of mine (a Mexican psychologist) insists that all pastoral agents must be involved as weekly participants in twelve-step recovery groups. I do not see codependency quite so widespread, but certainly such resources should be made available.

3. de la Rosa and Maw, *Hispanic Education.*

4. Of course, I do not mean to suggest that these problems are any more widespread among Latinos than among other communities. See Raul Ramirez's

article, "Violence at Home Grips Alien Women," in the *San Francisco Chronicle*, 10 March 1991, A1 and A20. He says that 34% of all undocumented Latina women in that area are survivors of domestic violence. A missionary sister in Mexico uses support groups in similar situations; when a spouse becomes abusive the wife bangs pots and pans and her group members come running to shame and denounce him publicly. She claims great success.

Bibliography

A.A. Worldservice. *Alcoholics Anonymous* (The Big Book). New York: A.A. Worldservice, 1986.

———. *A.A. and the Medical Profession.* New York: A.A. Worldservice, 1955.

Abad, V., and J. Suarez. "Cross-cultural Aspects of Alcoholism among Puerto Ricans." In *Proceedings of the Fourth Annual Alcoholism Conference of the National Institute on Alcohol Abuse and Alcoholism,* edited by M. Chafetz. Rockville, MD: NIAA, 1975.

Abalos, David T. *Latinos in the United States: The Sacred and the Political.* Notre Dame, IN: University of Notre Dame, 1986.

Adams, Walter Randolph. "Political and Economic Correlates of Pilgrimage Behaviors." *Anales De Antropologia* 20 (1983): 147–72.

Alcocer, A. M. "Alcohol Use and Abuse Among the Hispanic American Population." In *Alcohol and Health.* Rockville, MD: National Institute of Alcohol Abuse and Alcoholism, 1982.

———. "Chicano Alcoholism." Paper presented at the First Regional Conference of the Coalition of Spanish-Speaking Mental Health Organizations, Los Angeles, 1975.

———. "Quantitative Survey." In *Drinking Practices and Alcohol-Related Problems of Spanish-Speaking Persons in Three California Locales.* Prepared by Technical Systems Institute for the California Department of Alcohol and Drug Problems, 1979.

Alibardi, Lucinda A. *The Recovery Process in Alcoholics Anonymous: The Sponsor as Folk Therapist.* Ph.D. diss., University of California at Irvine, 1977.

Antze, Paul. "The Role of Ideologies in Peer Psychotherapy Organizations." *Journal of Applied Behavioral Sciences* 12 (1976).

Arredondo, R., R. Weddige, C. Justice, and J. Fitz. "Alcoholism in Mexican-Americans: Intervention and Treatment." *Hospital and Community Psychiatry* 38 (February 1987): 180–83.

Aymes, María de la Cruz, S.H. et al. *Effective Inculturation and Identity.* Rome: Pontifical Gregorian University, 1987.

Azevedo de Carvalho, Marcello, S.J. *Inculturation and the Challenges of Modernity.* Rome: Pontifical Gregorian University, 1982.

Babor, T. F., ed. *Alcohol and Culture.* New York: New York Academy of Sciences, 1987.

———. "Patterns of Alcoholism in France and America: A Comparative Study." In *Alcoholism: A Multilevel Problem,* edited by M. E. Chafetz. Washington, DC: U.S. Government Printing Office, 1986.

———, et al. "Ethnic-Religious Differences in the Manifestation and Treatment of Alcoholism." Paper presented at the Epidemiology Section meetings of the

27th International Institute on the Prevention and Treatment of Alcoholism. Vienna, June 1981.

Barbancho, Fernando Camara. "Santuarios y Peregrinaciones: Ensayo Sobre Tipologías Estructurales y Funcionales." In *Religión en Mesoamerica*, edited by J. L. King. México City: Instituto Nacional de Antropologia, 1972.

Bassin, Alexander. "Proverbs, Slogans, and Folk Sayings in the Therapeutic Community: A Neglected Therapeutic Tool." *Journal of Psychoactive Drugs* 16 (1984): 51–56.

Barkley, Roy. *The Catholic Alcoholic*. Huntington, IN: Our Sunday Visitor Press, 1990.

Bautista, Miguel Ramirez. *Comunidad Sin Fronteras*. Mexico City: Diana, 1986.

Blair, Bertha, Anne O. Lively, and Glen W. Trimble. *Spanish-Speaking Americans.* Homes Missions Research, 1959.

Blum, Richard. *Horatio Alger's Children: The Role of the Family in the Origin and Prevention of Drug Risk*. San Francisco: Jossey-Bass, 1972.

Borman, Leonard D. "Action Anthropology and the Self-Help/Mutual Aid Movement." In *Anthropology: Essays in honor of Sol Tax*, edited by R. Hinshaw. The Hague, Netherlands: Mouton Press, 1979.

Breve Diccionario Porrúa de la Lengua Española. Mexico City: Editorial Porrúa, 1989.

Buezas, Tomás Calvo. "Mitos, Rituales y Símbolos en el Movimiento Campesino Chicano." *Revista Española de Antropologia Americana* 11 (1981): 259–72.

Bullock, Jeffrey L. "Public Language, Public Conversion: Critical Language Analysis of Conversion and the History of Alcoholics Anonymous." *Saint Luke's Journal of Theology* 21 (March 1988): 127–41.

Burnam, Audrey. *Alcohol Use Among Mexican-Americans*. Washington, DC: National Institute of Alcohol Abuse and Alcoholism, 1990.

Burnam, M. A. "Prevalence of Alcohol Abuse and Dependence among Mexican-American and Non-Hispanic Whites in the Community." In *Alcohol Use Among U.S. Ethnic Minorities*, edited by D. C. Spiegler et al. Rockville, MD: National Institute on Alcohol Abuse and Alcoholism Research Monograph Number One, not dated.

Bushnell, John. "La Virgen de Guadalupe as Surrogate Mother in San Juan Atzingo." *American Anthropologist* 60 (1958): 261–65.

Cadena, Gilbert R. "Chicano Clergy and the Emergence of Liberation Theology." *Hispanic Journal of Behavioral Sciences* 11 (May 1989): 107–21.

Caetano, Raul. *Acculturation and Drinking Norms among U.S. Hispanics*. Berkeley, CA: Alcohol Research Group, Medical Research Institute of San Francisco, 1986.

———. *Acculturation, Drinking and Social Settings among U.S. Hispanics*. Berkeley, CA: Alcohol Research Group, Medical Research Institute of San Francisco, 1986.

———. *Acculturation, Drinking Patterns and Alcohol Problems among U.S. Hispanics*. Berkeley, CA: Alcohol Research Group, Medical Research Institute of San Francisco, 1986.

———. *Ethnic Minority Groups and Alcoholics Anonymous: A Review*. Berkeley, CA: Alcohol Research Group Publication B543, 1992.

———. *Patterns and Problems of Drinking among U.S. Hispanics*. Manuscript prepared under contract for the Department of Health and Human Services Task Force on Black and Minority Health, 1984.

———. "Reasons and Attitudes Toward Drinking and Abstaining: A Comparison of Mexicans and Mexican-Americans," *Community Epidemiology Work Group Proceedings.* Rockville, MD: NIDA, 1990.

———, and M. E. Medina-Mora. *Immigration, Acculturation and Alcohol Use: A Comparison between People of Mexican Descent in Mexico and in the U.S.* Berkeley, CA: Alcohol Research Group, Medical Research Institute of San Francisco, and Instituto Mexicano de Psiquiatria, 1986.

Cahalan, Don. *Understanding America's Drinking Problem.* San Francisco: Jossey-Bass, 1987.

———, I. Cisin, and H. Crossley. *American Drinking Practices.* New Brunswick, NJ: Rutgers Center of Alcohol Studies, Monograph No. 6, 1969.

———, R. Roizen, and R. Room. "Alcohol Problems and Their Prevention: Public Attitudes in California." In *The Prevention of Alcohol Problems: Report of a Conference,* edited by R. Room and S. Scheffield. Sacramento, CA: Office of Alcoholism, Health and Welfare Agency, 1974.

———, and B. Treiman. *Drinking Behavior, Attitudes and Problems in San Francisco.* Berkeley, CA: Alcohol Research Group, Medical Research Institute of San Francisco, 1976.

Campbell, Erna. "The Virgin of Guadalupe and the Female Self-Image: A Mexican Case History." In *Mother Worship: Themes and Variations,* edited by J. J. Preston. Chapel Hill: University of North Carolina Press, 1982.

Canals, Juan María, ed. *Nuevo Diccionario de Liturgia.* Madrid: Ediciones Paulinas, 1987.

Candelaria, Michael R. *Popular Religion and Liberation.* Albany: State University of New York Press, 1990.

Carrasco, Pedro. *El Catolicismo Popular de los Tarascos* Mexico City: SEPSETENTAS #298, 1976.

Castañeda, Carlos E. "Earliest Catholic Activities in Texas." *Catholic Historical Review* 17 (October 1931): 278–95.

Casté, C., and J. Blodgett. "Cultural Barriers in the Utilization of Alcohol Programs by Hispanics in the United States." In *Mental Health, Drug and Alcohol Abuse: An Hispanic Assessment of Present and Future Challenges,* edited by J. Szapocznik. Washington, DC: NCHMHHSO, 1979.

Centro de Estudios Guadalupanos, A.C. *Primer Encuentro Nacional Guadalupano.* Mexico City: Editorial Jus, 1978.

———. *Segundo Encuentro Nacional Guadalupano.* Mexico City: Editorial Jus, 1979.

Chafetz, Morris E., Harold W. Demone, and Harry C. Solomon, eds. *Alcoholism and Society.* New York: Oxford University Press, 1962.

Cinquino-Argana, Michael Anthony. *The Economic and Religious Organizations of a Mestizo Community in Western Mexico.* Ph.D. diss., State University of New York, Stony Brook, 1986.

Cohen, Lucy M., and Mary Ann Grossnicle, eds. *Immigrants and Refugees in a Changing Nation: Research and Training.* Washington, DC: Catholic University of America, 1983.

Condon, John C. *Good Neighbors: Communicating with Mexicans.* Yarmouth, ME: Intercultural Press, 1985.

Conlin, Sean. "Igualdad y Vergüenza." *Allpachis Phuturinga* 7 (1974): 143–62.

Cornelius, Wayne A. *Interviewing Undocumented Immigrants: Methodological Reflections Based on Fieldwork in Mexico and the United States.* San Diego: Working Papers on U.S.-Mexico Relations Number Two, 1981.

Costas, Orlando E. "Conversion as a Complex Experience," *Occasional Essays of the Latin American Evangelical Center for Pastoral Studies* 5 (1978): 21–43.

————. "Survival, Hope and Liberation in the American Church: A Hispanic Case Study." In *One Faith Many Cultures,* edited by W. E. Jerman. Maryknoll, NY: Orbis, 1988.

Cromwell, R. E., and R. A. Ruiz. "The Myth of Macho Dominance in Decision Making Within Mexican and Chicano Families." *Hispanic Journal of Behavioral Sciences* 1 (1979): 355–73.

Crumrine, N. Ross, and Barbara June Macklin. "Three North Mexican Folk Saint Movements." *Comparative Studies in Society and History* 15 (January 1973): 89–105.

Davis, Kenneth G. "A.A.: Making It User Friendly." *Apuntes* 10 (Summer 1990): 36–43.

————. "Base Communities: Changing the Chemistry of the Church." *Catholic World* 233 (1398) (November–December 1990): 281–85.

————. "Child Abuse in the Hispanic Community: A Christian Perspective." *Apuntes* 12 (Fall 1992): 127–36.

————. "Church Must Empower Chicanos." *East Bay Monitor* (November 1990): 7.

————. "CORHIM Hispanic Seminars." *Review for Religious* (November-December 1991): 881–87.

————. *Cuando el Tomar Ya No Es Gozar.* Los Angeles: Franciscan Communications Press, 1993.

————. "One Hundred and Twenty Five Years of Hispanic Presence in California Churches." *East Bay Monitor* (July 1989): 9.

————. "Return to the Roots: Conversion among the Mexican Descent." *Pastoral Psychology* 40, no. 3 (January 1992). 139–58.

————. "U.S. Hispanic Catholics: Trends and Recent Works 1992." *Review for Religious* 52 (March-April 1992): 283–303.

————. "We're Not in Kansas Anymore." *Priest* 46 (July 1990): 14–16.

Deck, Allan Figueroa, S.J. "The Hispanic Presence: A Moment of Grace." *Critic* 45 (Fall 1990): 48–59.

————, ed. *Frontiers of Hispanic Theology in the United States.* Maryknoll, NY: Orbis, 1992.

————. "Popular Culture, Popular Religion: Framing the Question." *Way Supplement* 73 (Spring 1992): 24–35.

————. *The Second Wave: Hispanic Ministry and the Evangelization of Cultures.* Mahwah, NJ: Paulist Press, 1989.

Denzin, Norman K. *Treating Alcoholism: An Alcoholics Anonymous Approach.* Newbury Park, CA: Sage, 1989.

Diaz, Frank. "Looking at Hispanic Ministry in 1987." *Austin Seminary Bulletin* 103 (1987): 37–42.

Dobkin De Rios, Marlene, and Daniel J. Feldman. "Southern Californian Mexican Drinking Patterns: Some Preliminary Observations." *Journal of Psychedelic Drugs* 9 (April–June 1977).

Eliade, M., ed. *The Encyclopedia of Religion.* New York: MacMillan, 1987.

Elizondo, Virgilio P. *Christianity and Culture.* San Antonio, TX: Mexican-American Cultural Center, 1975.

———. "Evil and the Experience of God." *The Way* 33 (January 1993): 34–43.

———. *The Future is Mestizo: Life Where Culture Meets.* Indiana: Meyer Stone Books, 1988.

———. *Galilean Journey: The Mexican-American Promise.* New York: Orbis, 1985.

———. "The Hispanic Catholic Church in the USA: A Local Ecclesiology." *Proceedings of the Catholic Theological Association* 36 (1981): 155–70.

———. "Mary and the Poor: A Model of Evangelizing Ecumenism." *Concilium* 168 (1983): 59–65.

———. *La Morenita: Evangelizadora de las Américas.* Missouri: Liguori, 1981.

———. "Popular Religion as Support of Identity: A Pastoral-Psychological Case Study Based on Mexican-American Experience in the U.S.A." *Concilium* (August 1986): 36–43.

———. "La Virgen de Guadalupe Como Simbolo Cultural." *Paginas* 10 (1977): 3–12.

Espín, Orlando. "God of the Vanquished: Foundations for a Latino Spirituality." *Listening* 27 (Winter 1992): 70–83.

———. "Grace and Humanness: A Hispanic Perspective." Paper presented at the Aquinas Conference *Somos Un Pueblo,* Emory University, Atlanta, GA, June, 1990.

Espinosa, Aurelio M. *The Folklore of Spain in the American Southwest.* Norman: University of Oklahoma Press, 1985.

Espinosa, Gilbert. "New Mexican Santos as Works of Art." *New Mexico Quarterly* 6 (May 1936): 182–89.

Galilea, Segundo. *The Future of Our Past.* Notre Dame, IN: Ave Maria Press, 1985.

———. *Pastoral Popular y Urbana en América Latina.* Bogotá, Colombia: CLAR, 1977.

———. "La Raiz de Nuestro Presente." *Christus* 41 (1976): 17–21.

———. *Religiosidad Popular y Pastoral Hispano-Americano.* New York: Centro Católico de Pastoral para Hispanos del Nordeste, 1981.

Gamio, Manuel. *Mexican Immigration to the United States: A Human Migration and Adjustment.* New York: Dover, 1971.

Garcia, Enrique Hugo. "Análisis Estructural de los Ritos Funerarios de San Miguel Aguasuelos, Veracruz." *La Palabra y el Hombre* 62 (Abril–Junio 1987): 15–21.

Garcia, Sixto J., and Orlando Espín. "'Lilies of the Field': A Hispanic Theology of Providence and Human Responsibility." *Proceedings of the Catholic Theological Association of America* 44 (1989): 74.

Geller, Anne. "Alcoholics Anonymous and the Scientific Model." In *Etiologic Aspects of Alcohol and Drug Abuse,* edited by E. Gottheil et al. Springfield, IL: Charles C. Thomas, 1983.

Gerhart, Piers. *Shame and Guilt: A Psychoanalytic and Cultural Study.* New York: Norton, 1971.

Gilbert, M. J. *Alcohol Consumption among Mexicans and Mexican-Americans: A Binational Perspective.* Los Angeles: University of California at Los Angeles, 1988.

―――. "Hispanic Americans: Alcohol Use, Abuse and Adverse Consequences." In *Alcoholism in Minority Populations,* edited by T. D. Watts and R. Wright. Springfield, IL: Charles C. Thomas, 1989.

―――. "Lifestyle Integration of Alcohol Consumption: Mexican-American and Anglo American Couples in a Southern Californian Community." Paper presented at the annual meeting of the American Psychological Association, LX, August 1987.

―――. "Mexican-Americans in California: Intracultural Behavior in Attitudes and Behavior Related to Alcohol." In *The American Experience With Alcohol: Contrasting Cultural Perspectives,* edited by L. A. Bennett and G. M. Ames. New York: Plenum, 1985.

―――, and R. C. Cervantes. "Alcohol Services for Mexican-Americans: A Review of Utilization Patterns, Treatment Considerations and Prevention Activities." *Hispanic Journal of Behavioral Sciences* 8 (1986): 191–223.

―――, and Ricardo Gonsalves. *The Social Context of Mexican and Mexican-American Male Drinking.* Los Angeles: Spanish Speaking Mental Health Research Center, 1985.

―――, Beatriz Sollis, and Juana Mora. *Alcohol-Related Issues in the Latino Population, 1980–1990: An Annotated Bibliography.* Berkeley, CA: Chicano Studies Library Publications, 1992.

Glazier, Mark. "La Muerte: Continuity and Social Organization in a Chicano Legend." *Southwest Folklore* 4 (1980): 1–13.

Goizueta, Roberto S. "Nosotros: Toward a U.S. Hispanic Anthropology." *Listening* 27 (Winter 1992): 55–69.

González, Roberto O., and Michael La Velle. "Cultural and Organizational Factors in the Delivery of Alcohol Treatment Services to Hispanos." *Working Papers on Alcohol and Human Behavior, No. 7.* Providence, RI: Dept. of Anthropology, Brown University, 1979.

―――. *The Hispanic Catholic in the United States: A Socio-Cultural and Religious Profile.* New York: Northeast Catholic Pastoral Center for Hispanics, 1985.

Gordon, Andrew J. "The Cultural Context of Drinking and Indigenous Therapy for Alcohol Problems in Three Migrant Hispanic Communities." *Journal of Studies on Alcohol* Supplement Number Nine (1981): 217–40.

Graves, T. D. "Acculturation, Access and Alcohol in a Tri-Ethnic Community." *American Anthropologist* 69 (1967): 306–21.

Greeley, A. M., W. C. McReady, and G. Theisen. *Ethnic Drinking Subcultures.* New York: Praeger, 1980.

Green, Judith Strupp, ed. *Death and Dying: Views from Many Cultures.* New York: Baywood, 1977.

Greil, Arthur L., and David R. Rudy. "Conversion to the World View of Alcoholics Anonymous: A Refinement of Conversion Theory." *Qualitative Sociology* 6 (Spring 1983): 5–27.

Greinacher, Norbert, and Norbert Mette. *Popular Religion.* Edinburgh: T. & T. Clark, 1986.

Guerrero, Andrés G. *A Chicano Theology.* New York: Orbis, 1987.

Guillet, David. "A Comparative View of the Role of the Fiesta Complex in Migrant Adaptation." *Urban Anthropology* 3 (1974): 222–42.

Hiebert, Paul G. "Conversion, Culture and Cognitive Categories." *Gospel in Context* 1 (1978): 24–29.

Isasi-Díaz, Ada María. "'Apuntes' for a Hispanic Women's Theology of Liberation." *Apuntes* 6 (Fall 1986): 61–70.

———, and Yolanda Tarango. *Hispanic Women: Prophetic Voice in the Church.* San Francisco: Harper and Row, 1988.

Jacobi, H. John. *Que Lejos Estoy . . . Religiosity and Urbanization of Mixteca Alta Migrants in Oaxaca City, Mexico.* Ph.D. diss., Pennsylvania State University, 1976.

Jacobs, Donald R. "Culture and the Phenomena of Conversion." *Gospel in Context* 1 (1978): 4–24.

Jessor, R., et al. *Society, Personality and Deviant Behavior: A Study of a Tri-Ethnic Community.* New York: Holt, Rinehart and Winston, 1968.

Johnson, L. V., and M. Matre. "Anomie and Alcohol Use: Drinking Patterns in Mexican-American and Anglo Neighborhoods." *Quarterly Journal of Studies on Alcohol* 39 (1978): 894–902.

Keefe, Susan K. *Emotional Support Systems in Two Cultures.* Los Angeles: Spanish Speaking Mental Health Research Center, 1978.

———, and Amando M. Padilla. *Chicano Ethnicity.* Albuquerque: University of New Mexico Press, 1987.

Kenaston, Monte R. "A Sketch of the History of Alcoholics Anonymous in Zacatecas, Mexico." Department of Anthropology, Memphis State University.

Kenney, Bradford P., et al. "Identifying the Socio-contextual Forms of Religiosity among Urban Ethnic Minority Group Members." *Journal for the Scientific Study of Religion* 16 (1977): 237–44.

King, Jaime L., ed. *Religión en Mesoamerica.* México City: Sociedad Mexicana de Antropologia, 1972.

Kleinman, Arthur. *Patients and Healers in the Context of Culture.* Berkeley: University of California Press, 1980.

Komonchak, Joseph A., et al. *The New Dictionary of Theology.* Wilmington, DE: Michael Glazier, 1987.

Kurtz, Donald V. "The Virgin of Guadalupe and the Politics of Being Human." *Journal of Anthropological Research* 38 (1982): 194–210.

Kurtz, Edward. *A.A.: The Story.* New York: Harper and Row, 1988.

———. *Not-God: A History of Alcoholics Anonymous.* Center City, MN: Hazelden, 1979.

Kurtz, Linda F. "Ideological Differences Between Professionals and A.A. Members." *Alcoholism Treatment Quarterly* 1 (1984): 73–85.

Kutsche, Paul. "Household and Family in Hispanic Northern New Mexico." *Journal of Comparative Family Studies* 14 (Summer 1983): 151–65.

Lampe, Phillip E. "Is the Church Meeting the Needs of Hispanics?" *Living Light* 27 (Fall 1990): 51–55.

Lang, Perry. "Targeting Minorities Assailed." *San Francisco Chronicle,* 10 December 1990: A1 and A12.

Latz, Alfred N., and Eugene I. Bender. "Self-Help Groups in Western Society." *Journal of Applied Behavioral Science* 12 (1976): 265–82.

Leavitt, Stewart B. *Social Issues and Communication of Myth in a Rescue Organization: Alcoholics Anonymous.* Ph.D. diss., Northwestern University, 1974.

Lender, Mark E. *Drinking in America: A History.* New York: Free Press, 1982.

Lieberman, Morton A., and Leonard D. Borman. *Self-Help Groups for Coping with Crisis.* San Francisco: Jossey-Bass, 1979.

Lockpez, Inverna, ed. *Chicano Expressions.* New York: Intar Latin American Gallery, 1986.

Lusero, G. T. *Alcoholics Anonymous in a Chicano Community: An Analysis of Affiliation and Transferability.* Ann Arbor, MI: University Microfilms, 1977.

Maccoby, M. "Alcoholism in a Mexican Village." In *The Drinking Man: Alcohol and Human Motivation,* edited by D. C. McClelland et al. New York: Free Press, 1972.

Madsen, W. *Mexican-Americans of South Texas.* New York: Holt, Rinehart and Winston, 1964.

————, and C. Madsen. "The Cultural Structure of Mexican Drinking Behavior." *Quarterly Journal of Studies on Alcohol* 30 (1969): 701–18.

Malone, Thomas, ed. *The Report of the Secretary's Task Force on Black and Minority Health.* Washington, DC: U.S. Department of Health and Human Services, 1986.

Mannion, Francis M. "Cultural Fragmentation and Christian Worship." *Liturgy 90* 21 (February/March 1990): 4–7.

Marcoux, Marcene. *Cursillo, Anatomy of a Movement.* New York: Lambeth, 1982.

Marin, Gerardo, and Raymond J. Gamba. *Expectations and Experiences of Hispanic Catholics and Converts to Protestant Churches.* Social Psychology and Laboratory Hispanic Studies Technical Report Number Two. San Francisco: University of San Francisco, 1990.

Markides, Kyriakos S. "Change and Continuity in Mexican-American Religious Behavior: A Three-Generation Study." *Social Science Quarterly* 65 (1984): 618–25.

Marshall, M., ed. *Beliefs, Behaviors and Alcoholic Beverages.* Ann Arbor: University of Michigan Press, 1979.

Martin, Greg. *The Gospel of Christ and the Gospel of A.A.: Divergent Paths of Human Liberation.* D.Min. diss., San Francisco Theological Seminary, 1983.

Martinez, Joe L., Jr., and Richard H. Mendoza. *Chicano Psychology.* 2d ed. San Diego: Academic, 1984.

Masi, Fidelia A. "Occupational Alcoholism." In *Mental Health, Drug and Alcohol Abuse: An Hispanic Assessment of Present and Future Challenges,* edited by J. Szapocznik. Washington: NCHMHHSO, 1979.

Matovina, Timothy. "Liturgy, Popular Rites and Popular Spirituality." *Worship* 63 (July 1989): 351–61.

Méndez, Veronica. *The Way Is Made in the Walking: The Formation of Hispanic Women in American Religious Communities.* Masters Thesis, Jesuit School of Theology at Berkeley, 1990.

Miller, Elaine K. *Mexican Folk Narratives from the Los Angeles Area.* Los Angeles: Publications of the American Folklore Society Memoir Series #56, 1967.

Misioneros del Espíritu Santo. *Santa María de Guadalupe.* Mexico City: San José del Altillo, 1981.

Mitchell, John Jr. *Critical Voices in American Economic Thought.* Mahwah, NJ: Paulist Press, 1989.

Moore, Joan. "The Death Culture of Mexico and Mexican-Americans." In *Death and Dying: Views from Many Cultures,* edited by Judith Strupp Green. New York: Baywood, 1980.

Muñoz, F. "Chicano Alcohol Counselor: A Donde Vamos?" In *El Uso de Alcohol: A Resource Book for Spanish-Speaking Communities,* edited by R. T. Trotter and J. A. Chavira. Atlanta: Southern Area Alcohol Education and Training Program, 1977.

National Conference of Catholic Bishops. *The National Pastoral Plan for Hispanic Ministry.* Washington, DC: USCC, 1987.

Neira, Gérman, S.J. "¿Tiene la Religión Una Función Alienadora?" *Christus* 40 (1975): 14–23.

Newman, Maria. "Charismatic Movement Gains Among Catholics." *The New York Times,* 1 March 1992: L28.

Ocampo Nieto, Jesús Ernesto. "Biblio-Hemerografía de las Fiestas y Ferias Populares y Tradiconales de México: 1885–1975." *Folklore Americano* 39 (1985): 91–132.

Orlandi, Mario A., ed. *Cultural Competence for Evaluators.* Rockville, MD: U.S. Department of Health and Human Services, 1992.

Ortiz, Isidro D. "Chicano Urban Politics and the Politics of Reform in the Seventies." *Western Political Quarterly* 37 (December 1984): 564–77.

Padilla, A.M., and P. Arranda. *Latino Mental Health: Bibliography and Abstracts.* Washington, DC: U.S. Government Printing Office, 1974.

Panitz, D. R., R. D. McConchie, R. Sauber, and J. A. Fonseca. "The Role of Machismo and the Hispanic Family in the etiology and treatment of Alcoholism in Hispanic American Males." *The American Journal of Family Therapy* 11 (1983): 31–44.

Parker, Christian. "Popular Religion and Protest against Oppression: The Chilean Example." *Concilium* (August 1986).

Peele, S. *The Meaning of Addiction: Compulsive Experience and Its Interpretation.* Lexington, MA: Heath, 1985.

Pérez, Arturo. *Popular Catholicism: A Hispanic Perspective.* Washington, DC: Pastoral Press, 1988.

Pescatello, Ann, ed. *Female and Male in Latin America.* Pittsburgh: University of Pittsburgh Press, 1973.

Petrunik, Michael G. "Seeing the Light: A Study of Conversion to Alcoholics Anonymous." *Journal of Voluntary Action Research* 1 (October 1972): 30–38.

Preston, James J., ed. *Mother Worship: Themes and Variations.* Chapel Hill: University of North Carolina Press, 1982.

Rachal, J. V., et al. *A National Study of Adolescent Drinking Behavior, Attitudes and Correlates.* Research Triangle, NC: Research Triangle Institute, 1975.

Rambo, Lewis R. "Conversion." In *Encyclopedia of Religion,* vol. 4, edited by M. Eliade. New York: MacMillan, 1987.

———. "Conversion: Toward a Holistic Model of Religious Change." *Pastoral Psychology* 38 (Fall 1989): 47–63.

Ramirez, Raul. "Violence at Home Grips Alien Women." *San Francisco Chronicle,* 10 March 1991: A1 and A20.

Ramirez, Ricardo. *Faith Expressions of Hispanics in the Southwest.* Vol. 1. San Antonio, TX: Mexican-American Cultural Center, 1979.

———. *Fiesta, Worship and Family.* San Antonio, TX: Mexican-American Cultural Center, 1981.

Regis Jesuit Community. *Santos and Saints: The Religious Folk Art of Hispanic New Mexico.* Sante Fe, NM: Ancient City Press, 1974.

Robinson, David. "The Growth of Alcoholics Anonymous." *Alcohol and Alcoholism* 18 (1983): 167–72.

Rodin, Miriam B. "Getting on the Program: A Biocultural Analysis of Alcoholics Anonymous." In *The American Experience with Alcohol,* edited by L. A. Bennett and G. M. Ames. New York: Plenum, 1985.

Rogers, Mary B. *Cold Anger: A Story of Faith and Power Politics.* Denton, TX: University of North Texas Press, 1990.

Rogler, L. H., et al. *A Conceptual Framework for Mental Health Research on Hispanic Populations.* New York: Hispanic Research Center, Fordham University, Monograph no. 10, 1983.

Roizen, R. *The World Health Organization Study of Community Responses to Alcohol-Related Problems: A Review of Cross-Cultural Findings.* Geneva: World Health Organization (Annex 41), 1981.

Romano V., Octavio Ignacio. "Charismatic Medicine, Folk-Healing and Folk-Sainthood." *American Anthropologist* 67 (October 1965): 1151–73.

Rootman, Irving, and Joy Moser. *Community Response to Alcohol Related Problems: A World Health Organization Project Monograph.* Washington, DC: World Health Organization, 1984.

Rosa, Denise de la, and Carlyle E. Maw. *Hispanic Education: A Statistical Portrait 1990.* Washington, DC: National Council of the Raza, 1990.

Rudy, David R., and Arthur L. Greil. "Is Alcoholics Anonymous a Religious Organization?: Meditations on Marginality." *Sociological Analysis* 50 (1988): 41–51.

Ruiz, Cortés Efaín. *The Days of the Dead: A Mexican Tradition.* Mexico City: GV Editores, 1988.

Sandoval, Moises, ed. *Fronteras: A History of the Latin American Church in the USA Since 1513.* San Antonio, TX: Mexican-American Cultural Center, 1983.

———. *On the Move: A History of the Hispanic Church in the United States.* New York: Orbis, 1990.

Sellner, Edward C. "What Alcoholics Anonymous Can Teach Us about Reconciliation." *Worship* 64 (July 1990): 331–48.

Siller A., Clodomiro. "Anotaciones y Comentarios al Nican Mopohua." *Estudios Indigenistas* 8 (1981): 217–74.

———. "Para Una Teología Del Nican Mopohua." *Servir* 12 (1976): 158–74.

Skansie, Juli Ellen. *Death Is for All: Death and Death Related Beliefs of Rural Spanish-Americans.* New York: AMS Press, 1985.

Spanish Speaking Mental Health Research Center. *Delivery of Services for Latino Community Mental Health.* Los Angeles: University of California at Los Angeles, Monograph Two, 1975.

———. *Emotional Support Systems in Two Cultures.* Los Angeles: University of California at Los Angeles Occasional Paper Number Seven, 1978.

———. *Psychotherapy with the Spanish-Speaking: Issues in Research and Service Delivery.* Los Angeles: University of California at Los Angeles Monograph Number Three, 1976.

Stevens, Evelyn P. "Marianismo: The other Face of Machismo." In *Female and Male in Latin America*, edited by A. Pescatello. Pittsburgh, Pa: University of Pittsburgh, 1973.

Subby, Robert. *Lost in the Shuffle*. Pompano Beach, FL: Health Communications, 1987.

Szapocznik, Jose, ed. *Mental Health, Drug and Alcohol Abuse: An Hispanic Assessment of Present and Future Challenges*. Washington, DC: Coalition of Spanish-Speaking Mental Health Organizations, 1987.

Taylor, William B. "The Virgin of Guadalupe in New Spain: An Inquiry into the Social History of Marian Devotion." *American Ethnologist* 14 (1987): 9–33.

Tiebout, Harry M. "The Act of Surrender in the Therapeutic Process." *Quarterly Journal of Studies on Alcohol* 10 (1949): 51–58.

———. "Alcoholics Anonymous—An Experiment of Nature." *Pastoral Psychology* 13 (April 1962): 45–57.

———. *Conversion as a Psychological Phenomenon*. New York: National Council on Alcoholism, not dated.

———. *Direct Treatment of a Symptom*. Center City, MN: Hazelden, not dated.

———. "Surrender versus Compliance in Therapy." *Quarterly Journal of Studies on Alcohol* 14 (March 1953): 58–68.

Tooker, Elisabeth. "The Pilgrims in Church." *Kiva* 16 (1950): 9–13.

Toor, Frances. *A Treasury of Mexican Folkways*. New York: Crown, 1947.

Trevino, M. E. "Machismo Alcoholism: Mexican-American Machismo Drinking." In *Proceedings of the Fourth Annual Alcoholism Conference of the National Institute on Alcohol Abuse and Alcoholism*. Rockville, MD: National Institute of Alcohol Abuse and Alcoholism, 1975.

Triacca, A. M. "Tiempo y Liturgia." In *Nuevo Diccionario de Liturgia*, edited by J. M. Canals. Madrid: Ediciones Paulinas, 1987.

Trice, Harrison M., and Paul M. Roman. "Sociopshychological Predicators of Affiliation with Alcoholics Anonymous: A Longitudinal Study of 'Treatment Success.'" In *Selection of Treatment for Alcoholics*, edited by M. E. Pattison. New Brunswick, NJ: Journal of Studies on Alcohol, 1982.

Turner, Kay F. "Mexican-American Home Altars." In *Chicano Expressions: A New View in American Art*, edited by I. Lockpez. New York: Latin American Gallery, 1986.

———. "Mexican-American Home Altars: Towards Their Interpretation." *Aztlan* 13 (1982): 309–26.

Turner, Victor, and Edith Turner. *Image and Pilgrimage in Christian Culture: Anthropological Perspectives*. New York: Columbia University Press, 1978.

Urrabazo, Rosendo. *Machismo: Mexican-American Male Self-Concept*, Ph.D. diss., Graduate Theological Union, Berkeley, CA, 1986.

Valdez, Facundo. "Vergüenza." *Colorado College Studies* 15 (Spring 1979): 99–106.

Vallen, R., and W. Vega, eds. *Hispanic Natural Support Systems: Mental Health Promotion Perspectives*. Sacramento: State of California, Department of Mental Health, 1980.

Vigil, Maurillio E. *The Hispanics of New Mexico: Essays on History and Culture*. Bristol, IN: Wyndham Hall, 1985.

Walter, James J. "Conversion." In *The New Dictionary of Theology*, edited by J. A. Komonchak et al. Wilmington, DE: Michael Glazier, 1987.

Weber, George H., and Lucy M. Cohen, eds. *Beliefs and Self-Help.* New York: Human Sciences, 1982.

Weigle, Marta. *The Lore of New Mexico.* Albuquerque: University of New Mexico Press, 1988.

West, Stanley A., and Macklin, June, eds. *The Chicano Experience.* Boulder, CO: Westview, 1979.

Williams, Peter W. *Popular Religion in America.* Englewood Cliffs, NJ: Prentice-Hall, 1980.

Wilson, Wilmer H. "Sobriety: Conversion and Beyond." *Maryland State Medical Journal* (April 1977): 85–91.

Wolf, Eric R. "The Virgin of Guadalupe: A Mexican National Symbol." *Journal of American Folklore* 71 (1958): 34–39.

Wyatt, Michael. "What Must I Believe to Recover? The Spirituality of Twelve Step Programs." *Quarterly Review* 9 (1989): 28–47.

Zazueta, Jesús Angel. *La Muerte y Los Muertos: Culto, Servicio, Ofrenda y Humor de Una Comunidad.* Mexico City: SEPSETENTAS #153, 1974.

Index